Volunteers
and Ministry

Volunteers and Ministry

A Manual for Developing Parish Volunteers

Sister Suzanne Donovan, S.C.
&
William J. Bannon

Paulist Press New York/Ramsey

All scripture quotations in this book are taken from *The Jerusalem Bible,* copyright © 1966 by Darton, Longman & Todd, Ltd. and Doubleday & Company, Inc., and are reprinted by permission of the publisher. All rights reserved.

Acknowledgement
The Publisher gratefully acknowledges the use of the following materials: material reprinted or adapted by permission from "Completing Volunteer Ministries;" "Supporting Volunteers;" "The Church and Its Volunteers;" "Training Volunteers" in the series The Ministry of Volunteers, © 1979, Office for Church Life and Leadership, United Church of Christ; excerpts from *Called and Gifted: The American Catholic Laity* copyright © 1980 by the Publications Office, United States Catholic Conference, Washington, D.C. are used with permission of the copyright owner.

Photographs by James Graham Photography, Columbus Ohio

Photograph locations: St. Peter's, Worthington, Ohio and Church of Our Lady, Columbus, Ohio

Library of Congress
Catalog Card Number: 82-62965

ISBN: 0-8091-2545-5

Published by Paulist Press
545 Island Road, Ramsey, N.J. 07446

Printed and bound in the
United States of America

CONTENTS

Preface

It can't have been over a year ago that we were invited to address the Pastoral Alliance at St. John Vianney Center in Steubenville, Ohio—but it was. We spent two days with a group of pastors who had invited us to share some parish management techniques with them.

At that session we concluded with a section on "How To Fire a Volunteer" and then gave the pastor a proposal covering possible future sessions. We waited down the hall as it was discussed.

Then Fr. Pat Maher came in and advised us that even after our session it was not easy to give us the bad news. After an appropriate pause he announced that the Alliance had accepted our proposal. Thus began a year-long association during which we shared many challenging and exciting hours with these priests who have committed themselves to change completely the meaning of the word parish and their roles as pastors.

This book is really a compilation of their work and ours during the last year. The Alliance will share in any profit it may generate.

We thank each of the pastors, Sister Carol Gross, the Executive Secretary of the Alliance, and Bishop Albert Ottenweller. They made their own lasting mark on us and on this work.

The reader should keep in mind that our writing is directed toward parishes embarking upon a course of staffing through volunteer leadership. Parishes with paid staff can use the same principles but should seek stronger accountability from staff.

All relationships covered are between the pastor and the staff people working directly with him. Once those relationships have been established, each minister should use the principle described here to bring his or her associates on board so that all parish volunteers will, eventually, have been recruited and trained with the same program.

William J. Bannon
S. Suzanne Donovan, S.C.

Acknowledgements

Grateful appreciation to. . . .

Most Reverend Albert Ottenweller, Bishop of Steubenville

The Priests of the Steubenville Pastoral Alliance: Reverend George Adams, Monsignor Frank Baudo, Reverend John Costlow, Reverend Walter Heinz, Reverend Charles Highland, Reverend Vincent Huber, Monsignor Edward Kakasick, Monsignor Lawrence Luciana, Monsignor Patrick Maher, Monsignor Paul Metzger, Monsignor Joseph Nealon and Reverend Dale Tornes

Sister Carol Ann Gross, O.P., Executive Secretary of the Pastoral Alliance who have been an inspiration and contributors to this manual

Patricia Pappangelis who edited the Manual

The countless members of the Alliance parishes who have implemented the concepts of this process

The Office of Church Life and Leadership of the United Church of Christ whose volunteer manual served as a tremendous resource

Introduction

Since Vatican II a wide variety of roles and responsibilities have emerged at parish and diocesan levels offering new and expanded opportunities for involvement by the laity.

This manual is based on the belief that every Christian because of baptism shares in the priesthood of Jesus Christ and, as such, has been given a special role or ministry as an extension of Jesus' ministry.

Further, we believe that ministry not only involves the good done by individuals or groups but also the attitude of Christ these works need to embody.

As people in parishes begin to work together to respond to the needs of their community in a true spirit of ministry the faith that compels that activity creates among them a sense of responsibility for one another. This was reflected in Scripture when the writer stated: "See how these Christians love one another." Today, we have begnn to call this experience building a faith community.

These following two sections present a focus on the individual and then the parish in beginning to develop volunteers in ministry.

I. Identifying Specific Ministries

"Having gifts that differ . . .
let us use them"
(Rom 12:6)

A. Perspective of Ministry

The story of God's revelation to his people began with Abraham and developed through the Old Testament to the coming of Christ. A parish reflects God's presence to the world, giving a significant expression of his continued love for his people. Each person bears a unique reflection of the Creator which comes to life in the community of faith. Parishioners are drawn to a special unity with one another in the faith community by virtue of baptism and sharing in the eucharistic life.

Our ability as Christians to give compelling witness to the active presence of the Spirit among us and to live the paschal mystery—life, death *and* resurrection—gives light and hope to a sometimes dismal society. As Jesus assures us, to know him is to know the Father, and in this knowledge we find the love that enables us to respond to the needs of our community, our parish, to embody the attitude that was Christ's in words and actions.

As a faith community, members of a parish grow in their awareness of being challenged by the Gospel to exercise the special gifts that enrich their lives in the development of the community. To give in his name, to give willingly, to do so in response to the needs of the community—this is ministry. Ministry such as this is not limited to ordination but rather is a call given to all of us in baptism.

The mission of the church is that of the Son of God to witness to His Father—to be his presence to his people—to make him known to all people.

> Just as a human body, though it is made up of many parts, is a single unit, because all these parts, though many, make one body, so it is with Jesus Christ. In this one Spirit we were all baptized, Jews as well as Greeks, slaves as well as citizens, and one Spirit was given to us all to drink. (1 Cor 12:12–13)

As an individual ministry reaches its fullness it is able to meet the needs of a parish community.

The following section expresses the basis of effective volunteer ministry as it extends to the parish itself.

Faith, Gift and Parish Vision

Faith gives clarity to the vision, meaning to the history, and the hope that ministers need to find meaning and purpose. The community, a gathering of faith-filled people, is replete with "faith responses" that give form to the vision. Each of us must encounter Christ in Scripture, in the lives of other parishioners and in the sacraments and then share that reality with others. God not only created in us the longing to know and love Him but gave us the ability to respond with those innate gifts and talents He bestowed on each of us, not for our sake, but for the sake of His people.

At times the talents and abilities of members of a parish are clear and well demonstrated, but at other times those gifts need to be nurtured and developed by, for, and in the community. Every person possesses gifts of ministry.

Individuals and the parish should prayerfully reflect on the needs of the community, to clarify the vision and to begin to discern the areas of ministry where the gifts of parishioners may be used or cultivated.

It is essential to discern the gifts of community members in openness and faith to call them to fruition and to affirm them in sharing responsibility for growth of the community.

Ministry serves the mission of the church and refers to the service of the community that expresses the living presence of Christ.

Diakonos, a Greek term, meaning one who serves, is basic to the concept of ministry. All who serve the community in the name of Christ, ordained or non-ordained, share in Christian ministry. Basic to all we do in community is: Why? Spirituality focuses our energies and our gifts, giving root and spirit to all we do as Church.

The Vatican II document on the laity states:

> The laity derive the right and obligation to the apostolate from their very union with Christ the head. Incorporated into Christ's mystical body by baptism and strengthened by the power of the

3

Holy Spirit in confirmation, they are assigned to the apostolate by the Lord himself. They are consecrated for the royal priesthood and the holy people (cf. 1 Pet 2:4–10) that they may offer spiritual sacrifices in everything and bear witness to Christ throughout the world.[1]

The American Catholic Laity - 1980[2]

The U.S. Bishops approved a set of pastoral reflections on the laity in the Church at their recent annual meeting in Washington. The reflections commemorate the 15th anniversary of the Second Vatican Council's Decree on the Laity. Bishop Albert Ottenweller, Steubenville, is chairman of the Bishops' Committee on the Laity, which prepared the document for presentation to the national meeting for approval. Reprinted with the permission of the United States Catholic Conference.

"PEOPLE OF GOD"

Among the most enduring contributions of the Second Vatican Council is its description of *the church as the people of God*. "This was to be the new people of God. For, those who believe in Christ, who are reborn not from a perishable but from an imperishable seed through the word of the living God (1 Pt 1:23), not from the flesh but from water, and the Holy Spirit (Jn 3:5–6) are finally established as 'a chosen race, a royal priesthood, a holy nation, a purchased people . . . you who in times past were not a people, but are now the people of God' (1 Pt 2:9–10)" (Lumen Gentium, 9).

This image, drawing on a rich biblical and historical tradition, gives marvelous expression to the role of the church as the sign of the kingdom of God. It was this kingdom which Jesus came to announce and to inaugurate by his life, death and resurrection. "After John's arrest, Jesus appeared in Galilee proclaiming the good news of God. 'This is the time of fulfillment. The reign of God is at hand. Reform your lives and believe the Gospel' " (Mk 1:14–16).

MANY DIMENSIONS

Jesus established the church to bear witness to God's kingdom especially by the way his followers would live as the people of God. "This is my commandment: Love one another as I have loved you" (Jn 15:12).

- The image of the people of God has many dimensions. Its meaning is best grasped through a variety of experiences. Each sheds light on the whole and enables us to appreciate and live it more deeply.

At the present time the light shed on the meaning of the people of God by the laity is especially noteworthy and exciting.

In an exercise of our charism of "bringing forth from the treasury of revelation new things and old" (LG, 25), we bishops praise the Lord for what is happening among the laity and proclaim as well as we can what we have been experiencing and learning from them.

While focusing on the laity, we wish to address the whole church.

- We affirm the vision of the Second Vatican Council and the importance it gives to the laity. We look forward to what is still to come under the guidance of the Holy Spirit, making the church more and more the perfect image of Christ.
- We also acknowledge that these continuing developments may require new concepts, new terminology, new attitudes and new practices.

In prayerful dialogue with all our sisters and brothers we are prepared to make those changes which will aid in building the kingdom.

THE CALL TO ADULTHOOD

As the Decree on the Apostolate of the Laity of Vatican II says:

- "Indeed, everyone should painstakingly ready himself or herself personally for the apostolate, especially as an adult.

"For the advance of age brings with it better self-knowledge, thus enabling each person to evaluate more accurately the talents with which God has enriched each soul and to exercise more effectively those charismatic gifts which the Holy Spirit has bestowed on all for the good of others" (*Apostolicam Actuositatem*, 30).

ADULT MEMBERS OF CHURCH

- One of the chief characteristics of lay men and women today is their growing sense of being adult members of the church.

Adulthood implies knowledge, experience and awareness, freedom and responsibility, and mutuality in relationships. It is true, however, that the experience of lay persons, "as church members'', has not always reflected this understanding of adulthood.

- Now, thanks to the impetus of the Second Vatican Council, lay women and men feel themselves called to exercise the same mature interdependence and practical self-direction which characterize them in other areas of life.

RESPONSE OF LAY PERSONS

We note the response of many lay persons to different opportunities for faith development. There is the "coming of faith in Jesus" and a strengthening of commitment to him and his mission which we commonly call evangelization. There is also the adult catechesis movement which allows persons to grow and deepen their faith, and there are those who in faith are seeking greater understanding through theological reflection.

- These and other adult lay persons have taken responsibility in their parish or diocese by serving in leadership positions on committees and boards.

ADULT CHRISTIAN LIVING

Adult Christian living is also noticeable, though not always as publicized, in the daily struggle to live out Christian values in family, neighborhood, school, government and work.

- This is a hopeful sign because the laity are uniquely present in and to the world and so bear a privileged position to build the kingdom of God there.

"You are the light of the world . . . Your light must shine before all so that they may see goodness in your acts and give praise to your heavenly Father" (Mt 5:14–16).

The adult character of the people of God flows from baptism and confirmation, which are the foundation of the Christian life and ministry. They signify initiation into a community of believers who, according to their state of life, respond to God's call to holiness and accept responsibility for the ministry of the church.

THE CALL TO HOLINESS

"*Thus it is evident to everyone that all the faithful of Christ of whatever rank or status are called to the fullness of the Christian life and to the perfection of charity. By this holiness a more human way of life is promoted even in this earthly society*" (LG, 40).

A UNIQUE CALLING

The Second Vatican Council clearly proclaimed the universal call to holiness.

- Not only are lay people included in God's call to holiness, but theirs is a unique call requiring a unique response, which itself is a gift of the Holy Spirit.

It is characteristic that lay men and women hear the call to holiness in the very web of their existence (LG, 31), in and through the events of the world, the pluralism of modern living, the complex decisions and conflicting values they must struggle with, the richness and fragility of sexual relationships, the delicate balance between activity and stillness, presence and privacy, love and loss.

RENEWAL MOVEMENTS

The response of lay people to this call promises to contribute still more to the spiritual heritage of the church. Already, the laity's hunger for God's word is everywhere evident.

- Increasingly, lay men and women are seeking spiritual formation and direction in deep ways of prayer. This has helped to spur several renewal movements.

CHALLENGE TO PARISH

These developments present a challenge to the parish because, for the most part, the spiritual needs of lay people must be met in the parish.

- The parish must be a home where they can come together with their leaders for mutual spiritual enrichment, much as in the early church: "They devoted themselves to the apostles' instruction and the communal life, to the breaking of bread and the prayers" (Acts 2:42).

EFFECT ON LITURGY

We call special attention to the effect this should have on liturgy. The quality of worship depends in great measure on the spiritual life of all present.

- As lay women and men cultivate their own proper response to God's call to holiness, this should come to expression in the communal worship of the church.

Simultaneously, as lay persons assume their roles in liturgical celebration according to the gifts of the Spirit bestowed on them for that purpose, the ordained celebrant will be more clearly seen as the one who presides over the community, bringing together the diverse talents of the community as gift to the Father.

- Whatever else the growing spiritual life of the laity entails, it certainly means a more intense sharing among the whole people of God of the gifts of the Spirit. And this we wish to reinforce.

THE CALL TO MINISTRY

"From the reception of these charisms or gifts, including those which are less dramatic, there arise for each believer the right and duty to use them in the church and in the world for the good of humankind and for the upbuilding of the church" (AA, 3).

Baptism and confirmation empower all believers to share in some form of ministry. Although the specific form of participation in ministry varies according to the gifts of the Holy Spirit, all who share in this work are united with one another. "Just as each of us has one body with many members, and not all members have the same function, so too we, though many, are one body in Christ and individually members one of another. We have gifts that differ according to the favor bestowed on each of us" (Rom 12:4–6).

- This unity in the ministry should be especially evident in the relationships between laity and clergy as lay men and women respond to the call of the Spirit in their lives.

The clergy help to call forth, identify, coordinate and affirm the diverse gifts bestowed by the Spirit. We applaud this solidarity between laity and clergy as their most effective ministry and witness to the world.

CHRISTIAN SERVICE: MINISTRY IN THE WORLD

"The laity, by their vocation, seek the kingdom of God by engaging in temporal affairs, and by ordering them according to the plan of God" (LG, 31).

Christian service in the world is represented in a preeminent way by the laity. It is sometimes called the "Ministry of the laity" and balances the concept of ministry found in the ecclesial ministerial services.

- Because of lay persons, Christian service or ministry broadly understood includes civic and public activity, response to the imperatives of peace and justice, resolution of social, political and economic conflicts, especially as they influence the poor, oppressed and minorities.

UNPRECEDENTED SITUATIONS

"The whole church faces unprecedented situations in the contemporary world and lay people are at the cutting edge of these new challenges.

It is they who engage directly in the task of relating Christian values and practices to complex questions such as those of business ethics, political choice, economic security, quality of life, cultural development and family planning.

Really new situations, especially in the realm of social justice, call for creative responses. We know that the Spirit moves in all the people of God, prompting the members according to their particular gifts and offices, to discern anew the signs of the times and interpret them boldly in the light of the Gospel.

- Lay women and men are in a unique position to offer this service.

RIGHTS AND RESPONSIBILITIES

"Just as by divine institution bishops, priests and deacons have been given through ordination authority to exercise leadership as servants of God's people, so *through baptism and confirmation lay men and women have been given rights and responsibilities to participate in the mission of the church.*

In those areas of life in which they are uniquely present and within which they have special competency because of their particular talents, education and experience, they are an extension of the church's redeeming presence in the world.

- Recognition of lay rights and responsibilities should not create a divisiveness between clergy and laity but should express the full range of the influence of the people of God. We see this and affirm it.

MINISTRY IN THE CHURCH

"As sharers in the role of Christ the priest, the prophet and the king, the laity have an active part to play in the life and activity of the church" (AA, 10).

- Since the Second Vatican Council new opportunities have developed for lay men and women to serve in the church.

We acknowledge gratefully the continuing and increasing contributions of volunteers and part-time workers who serve on parish and diocesan councils, boards of education, and financial, liturgical and ecumenical committees, as well as those who exercise roles such as special ministers of the eucharist, catechist and pastoral assistant.

• We are grateful, too, for the large numbers of lay people who have volunteered and are serving in the missions.

Growing numbers of lay women and men are also preparing themselves professionally to work in the church. In this regard religious sisters and brothers have shown the way with their initiative and creativity.

ECCLESIAL MINISTERS

"Ecclesial ministers, i.e., lay persons who have prepared for professional ministry in the church, represent a new development. We welcome this as a gift to the church. *There are also persons who serve the church by the witness of their lives and their self-sacrificing service and empowerment of the poor in works such as administration, housing, job development and education.*

• All these lay ministers are undertaking roles which are not yet clearly spelled out and which are already demanding sacrifices and risks of them and their families.

As lay persons increasingly engage in ecclesial ministry, we recognize and accept the responsibility of working out practical difficulties such as the availability of positions, the number of qualified applicants, procedures for hiring, just wages and benefits.

INCREASED ROLE FOR WOMEN

"Special mention must be made of women, who in the past have not always been allowed to take their proper role in the church's ministry.

• We see the need for an increased role for women in the ministries of the church to the extent possible.

We recognize the tensions and misunderstandings which arise on this question, but we wish to face these as part of a sincere attempt to become true communities of faith.

The combination of all these responses to the challenges of our times proclaims the interrelated oneness of ministry as a gift of the Spirit and we rejoice in this.

THE CALL TO COMMUNITY

"For from the wedlock of Christians there comes the family, in which new citizens of human society are born. By the grace of the Holy Spirit received in baptism these are made children of God, thus perpetuating the people of God through the centuries. The family is, so to speak, the domestic church" (LG, 11).

Most lay persons have a primary identification with family. This influences their expectations of and contributions to the church as the people of God. *The family, as a way of life, is often taken as a model for the church.*

In most families life is interdependent. Ideally, strengths and weaknesses are blended so that a growthful atmosphere is maintained.

And yet we must frankly admit that failure occurs, that in many families the ideal is not reached. For example, divorce and neglect are realities.

The parish has a vital contribution to make to all families struggling to be faith communities, for the parish can serve as a model and resource for families.

"Because lay women and men experience intimacy, support, acceptance and availability in family life, they seek the same in their Christian communities.

This is leading to a review of parish size, organization, priorities and identity. It has already led to intentional communities, basic Christian communities and some revitalized parish communities.

It is likely that this family characteristic of the laity will continue to influence and shape the community life of Christians. If it does, this should enable the clergy to give the kind of overall leadership which their office requires. Such trends are welcome in the church.

CONCLUSION

"The church is to be a sign of God's kingdom in the world. The authenticity of that sign depends on all the people: laity, religious, deacons, priests and bishops. *Unless we truly live as the people of God, we will not be much of a sign to ourselves or the world.*

We are convinced that the laity are making an indispensable contribution to the experience of the people of God and that the full import of their contribution is still in a beginning form in the post-Vatican II church.

We have spoken in order to listen. It is not our intention rigidly to define or control, to sketch misleading dreams or bestow false praise. We bishops wish simply to take our place and exercise our role among the people of God. We now await the next word."

Our Church and Volunteers

The following questionnaire[3] can be useful to stimulate thinking about the church's volunteer ministry program and to begin to identify parts of the program which might require attention or be a good place to begin making changes.

The questionnaire may be completed individually, but it probably will be more helpful for a group of leaders to complete it together so that they can work out consensus on each answer. If people disagree about an issue, it indicates that the church's needs to clarify its work in this area.

The following questions use VOLUNTEER to mean a person who does a task without financial compensation and without being forced to do it, VOLUNTEER MINISTRY to mean the ministry of Christians or the ministry of church members, a VOLUNTEER MINISTRY PROGRAM to mean a church's intentional planned work with its volunteers, and VOLUNTEER MINISTRY POSITION DESCRIPTION to mean written information about the purpose and activities of a volunteer ministry and expectations the church has of the person who does the ministry.

VISION OF THE CHURCH

YES   NO

1. Does your parish have a Vision Statement?
2. Has the Vision Statement been reviewed and either affirmed or revised in the past five years?
3. Is the Vision Statement regularly referred to as a guide and foundation for the parish programs and planning?
4. Are volunteers in the parish familiar with the Vision Statement?
5. Do volunteers understand how their ministry contributes to the Vision?
6. Does your parish regularly establish goals for its programs?
7. Who should decide if a Vision Statement needs to be developed or reviewed, and how it could be done? _____

_____

_____

VOLUNTEER MINISTRY POSITION DESCRIPTIONS

YES   NO

1. Is there a list of all volunteer ministry positions in the church?
2. Generally, do people have a good idea of what is expected of them when they accept a volunteer position?
3. Are there written position descriptions of at least 50% of the positions?

IDENTIFYING VOLUNTEERS

YES   NO

1. Are members of the council or staff aware of the gifts, talents and interests of most of the church members?
2. Is there any specific method for learning about interests and talents of new members?
3. Have most members of the church been given a specific or personal invitation to volunteer to do something that is suited to them?
4. Have most church members discussed with council or staff member what they would like to volunteer to do?
5. Is there any record kept which tells what church members would like to do or have been trained to do or have an interest in doing?

6. When persons complete a volunteer ministry, do they have an opportunity to explore new ways of volunteering? _____   _____

7. Who is, or could be, responsible for helping church members be aware of the gifts and interests of members so that suitable ministries can be chosen for them? _____

_____

_____

───

MATCHING VOLUNTEERS AND MINISTRY POSITIONS	YES	NO
1. Has every church member been given an opportunity for a volunteer ministry?	_____	_____
2. Has the volunteer work been shared by many members rather than by a few who have done most of the work over the years?	_____	_____
3. Has everyone changed, or had an opportunity to change, volunteer positions in the past three years?	_____	_____
4. Has everyone who is participating in a volunteer ministry been given a chance to discuss other possibilities for ministry for which he or she feels suited?	_____	_____
5. Can you say: "No one ever stopped participating because he or she simply wasn't interested or prepared to do the job"?	_____	_____
6. Is an effort made to make members aware of volunteer ministry opportunities in the community and beyond the local church?	_____	_____

7. Who is, or could be, responsible for deciding what members will be asked to undertake particular volunteer ministries? _____

_____

_____

_____

───

RECURITING VOLUNTEERS

	YES	NO

RECRUITING VOLUNTEERS

1. Is face-to-face conversation used for asking persons to serve in volunteer ministries?
2. Are persons being asked to take on a job given a written description of what they are being asked to do?
3. Is everyone who is asked to participate in a volunteer ministry given an accurate picture of how much time and effort it will take to carry it out?
4. Is everyone who is asked to participate in a volunteer ministry given information about what is needed to know in order to do the ministry well?
5. Have all church members been given a choice of volunteer ministry positions?
6. Are persons told why they were chosen to be asked to undertake a particular volunteer ministry?
7. Who is, or could be, responsible for recruiting members for ministry positions within our parish? _____

_____

_____

_____

SUPPORTING VOLUNTEERS

	YES	NO

1. Do all volunteers receive orientation and training for their tasks so they can go about them with confidence and work effectively?
2. Do all volunteers know there is someone available to assist and encourage them?
3. Generally, are parish members aware of persons doing volunteer ministry on their behalf in the community and beyond the local parish?
4. Are volunteers recognized and thanked by the parish for their services?
5. Do volunteers have adequate resources to carry out their work?
6. Are records kept of the volunteer services of each member?
7. Who is, or could be, responsible for supporting volunteers? _____

_____

_____

COMPLETING A VOLUNTEER MINISTRY

	YES	NO
1. When people undertake a volunteer ministry do they know how long it will last?		
2. Is it possible to take on a volunteer position in the parish "for life" without renewing the commitment from time to time?		
3. When the volunteer ministry is completed does the volunteer have an opportunity to discuss how it went, what was accomplished, what was learned and what the frustrations were?		

EVALUATING THE VOLUNTEER MINISTRY

	YES	NO
1. Is there a designated group of persons whose responsibility it is to evaluate the church's volunteer ministry?		
2. Have volunteers been given an opportunity to express their feelings about the work and to suggest changes in the program?		
3. What is the rate of turnover?		
4. Is evaluation seen by the parish as a way to improve and work for greater excellence rather than as criticism?		

B. Methods in Determining Ministerial Needs of a Parish

Before parishioners attempt to outline the job responsibilities of ministry volunteers, time should be spent in determining the ministerial needs of a parish. Several approaches are presented so that a parish may follow the process that best accomplishes the task.

In this section, several ways to identify the areas of need in ministry are suggested. Each of the procedures has value and has been successfully employed.

1. Vision Process

Within the parishes themselves, pastors with groups of lay leaders focus on five questions in order to come to a statement of their vision of parish.

1. What are our assumptions?

2. What does Scripture tell us?

3. What does our history tell us?

4. What does recent scholarship on Church tell us?

5. How do we want to summarize and state our vision?

Parishes may engage in consultation via questionnaires for the entire parish or may seek input from various groups such as RENEW groups, Christ Renews His Parish, parish council and others. Writing committees collate, summarize and write a statement for the approval of the group who have participated in the Vision sessions.

Ministry flows from Vision. It is probable, therefore, that the ministerial needs are stated in the Vision and can be listed with appropriate parish level subgroupings or activities.

WRITING A PARISH VISION
Question 1: What are our assumptions concerning our parish?

The purpose of this session is to introduce the process and to begin discussing the present state of the parish.

Get-acquainted activities are very important to a newly organized group so that people learn one another's names and begin to feel more at ease.

Overview of purpose and components of entire process.

1. The purpose is to clearly state:

- What the parish is like now.
- What people feel they are called by the Lord to become.
- The gap between.

2. Questions to be considered:

- What are our assumptions?
- What is our history?
- What does Scripture say about forming a people?
- What does the universal Church say about itself?
- How do we summarize our Vision of the parish?

Faith Experience—Who is my God?

Our understanding of who God is and the way we relate to him has much to do with our views of everything else.

1. On small sheets of paper, one to a paper, write as many names for God as the group can think of.

2. When this is completed, each person selects one name for God—the one he or she relates to best.

3. Write a short prayer expressing your relationship with God, using the name you picked to begin the prayer.

4. Using Mt 16:13–18, have a short prayer service using the prayers of each person.

Brainstorming—What are our assumptions?

As quickly as possible, each person writes three conclusions to each of these sentences:
Our parish is . . .
The people in our parish should . . .
Our priests and sisters should . . .
Our parish should try to become . . .

Groups of four or five collate all answers on large sheets of paper. Post all papers for general discussion of commonalities, areas of agreement and disagreement. Keep papers for later session.

Summarizing

Time permitting or as homework: Each person individually describes his or her parish—the good things and the challenges it faces.

Either collect anonymously and type all of the responses to be distributed at next session or collect and read them now or have each person read his or her own or (if done for homework) do one of the above at next session.

The next session will explore the spirit and tradition of your parish history. Bring any material that may be helpful for this—Jubilee Books, photographs, etc.

Option: Pass out a two or three page summary of American church history.

Question 2: What is our history as a parish?

The purpose of this session is to reflect on the history of the parish as a whole and our own personal history of being in any parish. This will give us a sense of continuity with the traditions that help make the parish what it is.

Opening Prayer/Scripture Prayer—Reflection

Personal Parish History (to be shared in groups of four or five, one question at a time)

- What were your first impressions of this parish?
- When did you really begin to feel a part of the parish? Was there a particular occasion?
- Has the parish helped in your formation? How? If not, why do you feel it has not?

Story of the Parish

Use the written history of the parish from the pastor or the person most familiar with it, to tell the story of the parish.

Or

On a large paper, work together on a time line that shows significant events and milestones. Then try to determine the following:

1. What was the early spirit of the parish?

2. What was the mission of the parish? Did that change through its history?

Implications for our parish vision

List on large sheets.

Looking at the personal history of the parish and the parish story, what elements from the past do we want to include in our vision of the future? What do we want to hold on to or restore?

Question 3: What does Scripture say about forming a people?

The purpose of this session is to reflect prayerfully on God's call to us to form a people. Old and New Testament passages are used to focus in on the ideal parish community.

Short Opening Prayer

As deemed appropriate for the group, present a method of reflecting on Scripture.

One possible method is based on six P's:

Passage—Pick a passage to reflect upon

Place alone—Find a place where you will be least distracted or disturbed

Posture—For meditation of this kind, most people prefer to sit in an alert but relaxed position

Presence of God—Awareness, Acknowledgement, Rest

Purpose of Prayer—Express this consciously, i.e., For God's guidance, To give him praise, To come to a particular grace

Passage from Scripture—Read slowly and reflectively; perhaps read several times

Give 15–30 minutes of quiet time to reflect on a passage on church, using above method (may go to church for this part).

Small group sharing—What this passage says to me about our parish.

Decide on elements to be reflected in Vision.

Large group sharing of elements of Vision

Write Vision of parish based on these elements, time permitting.

Sharing of this Vision with entire group within context of closing prayer.

Read Scripture: Habakkuk 2:1–3

Read statements individually. Sing a familiar hymn.

Possible passages for reflection:

Exodus 24:1–9

Leaders of the Israelites seal a covenant with God

John 15

Jesus is the vine—no slave is greater than his master

Acts 2

Spirit comes to inspire apostles—birthday of the Church

Acts 6:1–7

Choosing deacons—administration and division of community work

Acts 9:1–31

The conversion of Paul and his early trials

1 Corinthians 12

Call to community—one body of Christ

1 James 2:14–18
Faith and actions—service of others
Question 4: What does the universal Church say about itself?

The purpose of this session is to broaden understanding of possible ways to look at Church. This is done through exploring Dulles' models of Church.

Prayer—Reflection on a Scripture passage, petitions of things needed for the good of the parish.
Questionnaire—Whatsit?[4]
Answer individually
Discussion of answers
Group scoring
Presentation—Short simple presentation on the models of Church; Avery Dulles, *The Models of the Church.*[5]

Break into small groups—one for each model
Answer these questions:

- What would the parish be trying hardest to accomplish if this were the predominant model?
- What attitudes, activities, programs or ways of doing things are characteristic of your parish right now that show the presence of this model?
- If this model were the predominant view of this parish, how would the sacraments, liturgy, weddings, and funerals be celebrated? What would the parish council be like?
- If this model were predominant, what would the people expect the pastor and staff to be and to do?
- What from this model would you most like to see included in your Vision?

Put the answers to the last question on large sheets for last session.
Final preparation for Vision forming and discernment sessions

Be sure everyone knows that he or she will be asked to think of descriptions of the parish/what it is called to be. A form could be given such as:

Describe your present experience of parish in relation to attitudes, people, community, prayer, programs—anything that tells about your parish—good, bad or indifferent.	What are your hopes and dreams? What would you like your parish to be?

Question 5: How do we summarize our Vision of the parish?

The purpose of this meeting is to summarize our understanding of who we are as a parish and who we are called to become.
Opening prayer—Scripture reflections, hymns, prayers of praise and thanksgiving.

Post and reread from first four questions.

Using these as reference and material from forms given out the week before, each person lists present experience of parish and future dreams for it.

Post papers or, if the group is larger than ten, share papers in small groups.

Determine three to six major areas under which others could be grouped. Each person then can classify each of the points by using code letters assigned to major areas.
Discuss options on how to proceed
1. Write Vision with this input

2. Ask other parishioners for input (optional)

3. Sunday questionnaire

4. Parish meeting—open to all

5. Parish council

6. Groups or organizations within the parish
Prepare time line on when statement should be completed.
Explain what comes next

Writers come back to group for approval and general appearance of statement. Commitment of this group to it. Proclamation to parish at large. Closing prayer and celebration.

2. Needs Assessment Process

After particularly the first year in the development of the Vision, an assessment may be helpful to identify the current and future needs of the parish.
Step 1: A committee is convened whose:

TASK is to reflect on the progress in ministry over the past year and develop priority ministerial needs for the coming year. Several things should be kept in mind:

(a) These ministries may be exactly the *same* as those stated at the outset.

(b) The list may be the same but the order may change.

(c) No ministry should be undertaken that is not reflected in the Vision.

MEMBERSHIP The members of the committee should include the pastor, staff, ministry team, parish council and others as appropriate to the parish. Be sure this committee is reflective of the entire parish and not limited to the "activists."

Step 2: Process for Needs Assessment

(a) The group should first spend an evening of reflection and prayer reviewing the Vision Statement, models of Church and *Called and Gifted* as well as other appropriate documentation.

(b) The committee team brainstorms a list of strengths, positive growth indicators, and new developments in the past year. These are listed on newsprint and posted so that all may reflect on them.

(c) Each member is asked to take ten minutes to list individually the ministerial needs of the parish and community as he or she and the group he or she represents see them.

(d) After sufficient time a combined list is made and posted.

(e) These needs are discussed so that all are able to agree and then are prioritized so that those presented to the representative groups are presented to reflect greatest needs first.

(f) Goal setting, time and talent surveys, etc., are then able to be developed based on existing and current needs.

3. *Profiling a Developing Parish*

This profile is adopted from *The Parish Development Process*[6] by Marvin T. Judy and *Hope Is an Open Door*[7] by Mary Luke Tobin.

The following developmental process is suggested for use in the parish after at least two years of active participation in both Vision development and volunteer ministry implementation. Those who take part in the following process should be representative of the entire parish: staff, volunteer and/or paid, parish council, committees and organizations, activists as well as the less obvious participants. The Vision Statement should be reflected upon at the end of the process.

The level, time and nature of participation will be determined by the committee formed from the ministerial team in Step 2.

STEP 1: The profile begins with an examination of the present development in parish, critical areas of community life, leadership and action.

STEP 2: A committee representative of the existing ministerial team should be convened. The size of the group will be dictated by the size of the parish and organizational structure. The task of the committee is to review the parish profile and validate existing ministries while also looking toward areas where ministry leadership may need to be developed.

STEP 3: The following is a suggested process.

PARISH PROFILE FOR A DEVELOPING PARISH

I Community Life—This part of the profile seeks to understand the impact the parish has on the community life of its parishioners. The impact will be examined from eight areas: renewal, liturgical, educational, ministerial, prophetic, social justice, neighborhood, and global involvement. It would be helpful for the entire profile team to come to a clear understanding about the definition of each of these terms so that there will be consistency in the final project. In each of these areas the process will be to examine if the parish has an impact, in what ways (documentation), and a determination of that impact. In responding to questions, keep in mind that in this section we are dealing with the community life of the total parish.

A. *Renewal*

1. Has renewal had an impact on the parish community?

2. In what ways has renewal affected the life of the community? (be specific)

3. What has been the impact of renewal?

4. Who has been affected by the renewal process?

B. *Liturgy*

1. Has the liturgical life of the parish had an impact on the parish community?

2. How has the liturgical life of the parish had an impact on the parish community?

3. What has been the effect of the liturgical life on the parish community?

4. Who has been affected by the liturgical life of the parish?

C. *Education*

1. Has education had an impact on the parish community?

2. How has education affected the parish community?

3. Whom in the parish community has education impacted?

4. What has been the effect of education on the life of the parish community?

D. *Ministry*

1. Have various ministries had an impact on the parish community? (ministry to the divorced, aged, youth, sick, etc.)

2. In what ways has ministry affected the parish community?

3. Who in the parish community has been ministered to?

4. What has been the effect of ministry on the parish community?

E. *Prophet*

1. Has the prophetic role had an impact on the parish community?

2. How has the prophetic stance had an impact on the parish community?

3. Who in the parish community has been affected by the prophetic role?

4. What has been the impact of the prophetic stance on community life of the parish?

F. *Social Justice*

1. Has the issue of social justice had an impact on the life of the parish community?

2. How has social justice affected the parish community?

3. Who in the community has been impacted by the issue of social justice?

4. What has been the impact of social justice on the parish community?

G. *Neighborhood*

1. Has the neighborhood had an impact on the life of the parish community?

2. Has the parish community had an impact on the neighborhood?

3. How has the neighborhood had an effect on the life of the parish community?

4. How has the parish community had an effect on the neighborhood?

5. What has been the impact of the neighborhood on the life of the parish community?

6. What has been the impact of the parish community on the neighborhood?

H. *Global Involvement*

1. Has the issue of global involvement had an effect on the parish community?

2. How has global involvement affected the life of the community?

3. Who in the community has been affected by the issue of global involvement?

4. What has been the impact of global involvement on the life of the parish community?

In order to complete these eight sections, a recommended approach would be to divide the work into eight parts and ask each group to deal with its section from the vantage point of community life, leadership and action, so that when the examination is finished, each section would have a report that covered the issue from three areas of interest. The process recommended for achieving the necessary information would be to interview a broad cross-section of the parish community, including parish staff and leaders.

II Leadership—This section of the profile focuses on the recognized leaders in the parish. Its aim is to examine if, how, and what effect renewal, liturgy, education, ministry, prophet, social justice, neighborhood, and global involvement have had on the formation of the parish leaders. This section can be completed by asking the leaders to respond to the questions in each section and turning that information over to the committees working on those sections.

A. *Renewal*

1. Has renewal had an impact on you as a leader?

2. How has renewal affected your leadership?

3. What has been the effect of renewal on you as a parish leader?

B. *Liturgy*

1. Has liturgy had an effect on your formation as a leader?

2. How has liturgy impacted your leadership?

3. What has been the effect of liturgy on you as a parish leader?

C. *Education*

1. Has parish education had an effect on your formation as a parish leader?

2. How has parish education impacted your leadership?

3. What has been the effect of education on you as a parish leader?

D. *Ministry*

1. Has the parish ministry had an effect on your formation as a parish leader?

2. How have the different parish ministries impacted your leadership?

3. What has been the effect of the various ministries on you as a parish leader? (please be specific regarding which ministries)

E. *Prophet*

1. Has the prophetic stance had an effect on your formation as a parish leader?

2. How has the role of prophet impacted your leadership?

3. What has been the effect of the prophetic role on you as parish leader?

F. *Social Justice*

1. Have social justice issues had an effect on your formation as a parish leader?

2. How has social justice impacted your leadership?

3. What has been the effect of social justice issues on you as a parish leader?

G. *Neighborhood*

1. Has the neighborhood had an effect on your formation as a parish leader?

2. How has the neighborhood impacted your leadership?

3. What has been the effect of the neighborhood on your formation as a parish leader?

H. *Global Involvement*

1. Has global awareness had an effect on your formation as a parish leader?

2. How has global involvement impacted your leadership?

3. What has been the effect of global awareness/involvement on you as a parish leader?

There may be areas where there has been no impact on the parish leadership. This would reflect the present condition of the parish. If there is concern that these issues be reflected in the continued development of the parish, that should be included in the mission statement along with a plan for how that can be accomplished.

III Action—This part of the profile seeks to examine the actions this parish takes, which, when examined from the point of view of each one of the eight areas, will reflect the present priorities of the parish, whether proclaimed or not. For example, if the parish proclaims to focus on adult education and yet, in effect, when the actions are examined only four adult classes are held during the year which affect only a few people, then obviously, although it proclaims adult education as a priority, in action it is not. Another example might be the belief that the parish has a positive effect on the neighborhood, but, when examined, it is not reflected as important in the community life or leadership of the parish. The sections on community life and leadership are valuable resources for this section along with the actual parish functions, meetings, committees, etc. This section aims to substantiate the present development in the parish.

A. *Renewal*

1. In the past two years, what actions have been aimed at renewing the parish?

2. How many people were involved?

3. How much money was spent?

B. *Liturgy*

1. In the past two years, what actions have been aimed at the continued development of the liturgical life of the parish? (This would not include the scheduled Sunday Masses, but would include the development of a liturgy committee, the development of a choir or guitar group for a particular Mass, or the development of an RCIA program.)

2. How many people are involved?

3. How much money was spent?

C. *Education*

(if there is a school and a religious education program, give separate figures for each one)

1. In the past two years, what actions have been aimed at:

(a) Adult education

(b) Young adult education

(c) Youth education

(d) Elementary education
(e) Pre-school education

2. How many people were involved in:
(a) Adult education
(b) Young adult education
(c) Youth education
(d) Elementary education
(e) Pre-school education

3. How much money was spent on:
(a) Adult education
(b) Young adult education
(c) Youth education
(d) Elementary education
(e) Pre-school education
D. *Ministry*
1. In the past two years, what actions have been aimed at the development of different ministries within the parish? (Please be specific, i.e., ministry to the aged, divorced, youth, family.)

2. How many people were involved and in what area of ministry?

3. How much money was spent?
E. *Prophet*
1. In the past two years, what actions have been aimed at understanding and promoting prophetic activity within the parish?

2. How many people were involved?

3. How much money was spent?
F. *Neighborhood*
1. In the past two years, what actions have been aimed at involvement and development of the neighborhood?

2. How many people were involved?

3. How much money was spent?
G. *Global Involvement*
1. In the past two years, what actions have been aimed at the awareness of and need for global involvement?

2. How many people were involved?

3. How much money was spent?
After completing the reports in each of the eight areas, the Vision Statement should be reviewed. It should reflect the future development of the parish in light of the present priorities and development. A process of establishing goals and objectives should be initiated from which it is possible to develop a 3–5 year Parish Plan.

BIBLIOGRAPHY

Suggested Readings for Leadership Development in Parish Communities
Parish Council Handbook, Diocese of Steubenville, Ohio.
Parish Council Handbook, Diocese of Columbus, Ohio.
Strategy Booklet, Coordinator of Parish Councils, Diocese of Steubenville.
A Model of the Church in Ministry and Mission, The Center for Parish Development, Naperville, Illinois.
Spiritual Growth: Key to Parish Renewal, Earnest Larsen, Liguori Publications, Liguori, Missouri.
Parish Life: Manual for Spiritual Leadership Formation, Sister Nancy Westmeyer, O.S.F., Paulist Press, Ramsey, New Jersey, 1983.
Mutual Ministry, James Fenhagen, The Seabury Press, New York, 1977.
Theological Models for the Parish, Sabbas J. Killian, O.F.M., Alba House, New York, 1977.
The Ministering Parish, Robert R. Newsome, Paulist Press, Ramsey, New Jersey, 1982.
Traditions, Tensions and Transitions in Ministry, William J. Bausch, Twenty-Third Publications, Mystic, Connecticut, 1982.

C. Typical Ministerial Needs

In an attempt to offer a bit of order to any effort to organize all the ministerial activities of a parish community, we selected the following seven key areas with brief descriptions of the scope of this ministry. This does not preclude the ability of a parish to add or delete in accordance with its needs but in fact offers a beginning catalogue as resource.

Suggested Ministerial Needs

1. *Temporal Ministry*—involves all parish resources, parish budget, parish support and the effective use and maintenance of parish facilities and properties. The ministry should also be concerned with personnel, records and general parish organization.
2. *Religious Ministry*—involves the coordination and organization of an ongoing religious program which effectively addresses the needs of the various groups in the parish community from birth till death.
3. *Social, Recreational and Ecumenical Ministry*—involves all activities that seek to respond to the human needs or human rights of people of every age. The ministry effectively establishes ties between our brothers and sisters of other religious affiliations and attempts to coordinate efforts that unify and heal.
4. *Youth Ministry*—involves youth, young adults and all who minister to them in developing the spiritual, social and service dimension of their lives.
5. *Spiritual Development Ministry*—involves a variety of means for individual spiritual growth and deepening of the faith community of the parish as a whole. The ministry involves all aspects of spirituality from the support services and resources to the establishment of programs and projects.
6. *Liturgical Ministry*—involves and trains a group of people to prepare and assist in carrying through Sunday liturgies and special celebrations in all aspects to enrich the sacramental life of the total congregation.
7. *Clerical Ministry*—addresses the general business procedures in the parish, particularly typing, filing, record keeping and basic accounting. The support and compassion of listening and encouraging as well as parish confidentiality are basic ministry traits.

II. Leadership Identification

As the parish initiates the process of identifying people who are interested in and able to be involved in volunteer ministry, specific processes are helpful in canvassing the parish community. This section presents several possible ways to identify potential ministry volunteers.

Preparing for the Time and Talent Survey

A Model

As with all of the material in the manual, we are proposing one possible way to handle the time and talent surveying. Each parish will need to modify this to meet the specific needs and nature of the parish.

STEP 1

At least two weeks before the survey actually occurs the pastor should distribute a letter to all parishioners. A suggested format is enclosed. The nature of the letter is to suggest to parishioners that the parish is looking for their assistance, that is essential to the growth of the community and that there will be time spent during the liturgy discussing this with them.

STEP 2

The week before the survey is taken, there should be an announcement in the bulletin. A suggested format is enclosed in the manual. The purpose is to capture the attention and interest of the parish.

STEP 3

The week before the survey, it would also be helpful to enclose a copy of the survey labeled SAMPLE in the bulletin so that parishioners may study the form and consider what gifts there are which reflect talents they are willing to share.

STEP 4

The Sunday before the survey, the pastor or his representative should spend time within the homily discussing the nature of the survey, why each adult has a responsibility to share his or her talents, and how the survey will be conducted.

STEP 5

Surveys are distributed at the liturgy on a given Sunday. Parishioners are asked to complete them at their convenience, drop them at the rectory or return them at next Sunday's liturgy. Envelopes may be attached to the survey for mailing but this tends to be expensive. Three Sundays are provided for follow-up.

STEP 6

A group is convened (staff and/or council) which will tabulate the surveys. This should be completed in a categoric manner so that under each group subheadings are listed with names, addresses and phone numbers. These should be typed and a master kept in the rectory with the sub-lists given to the person who is responsible for that ministry.

STEP 7

All those who volunteered should be contacted by phone within two weeks of the compilation of the data. A general thank you should appear in the bulletin and the newsletter and a comment should be included in the remarks the priest makes during liturgy.

STEP 8

The process ideally should be repeated every two years, depending on the nature of the parish.

STEP 9

New parishioners' packets or information given to new parishioners should include a Time and Talent Survey.

NOTE

The personal discernment that is inherent in the process is based in the belief that what is done in his name rises from a spirit and life of prayer.

Suggested procedures for discernment:

1. Gather the family or friends in prayer. You might read Matthew 25:14–20, reflect in silence, and share its meaning with one another.

2. Read the Parish Vision Statement and share its meaning with one another.

3. Place first name or initial after your "commitments."

4. Have each family member discuss his or her specific interest and discuss as a group the reality of family and personal involvement.

5. Make final determination reflecting primary responsibilities to the family and home as well as the generosity of giving.

6. Conclude with a prayer.

Letter from Pastor

My Dear Parishioners:

On the weekend of _____, our parish will initiate a Time and Talent Program. It is an appeal to parishioners to share responsibility in parish ministries as Vatican II has urged. As a parishioner, you will be asked to volunteer some of your personal time and talent to various lay ministries in a spirit of shared ministry.

The Time and Talent Program consists of two parts: preparation and implementation.

Next weekend's homily will ask you to be specific and select a ministry you intend to perform regularly. You will then sign a commitment card stating your intention. Your card will be filed in the rectory and you will be contacted later.

To help you understand the whole range of shared ministries, a master list is enclosed which specifies most of the ministries in the parish. The ministries chosen for the commitment card will be peculiar to this parish. They will be selected from the master list.

I sincerely seek your cooperation in this Time and Talent Program. You are blessed with a special talent for ministry. This program in ministry is asking you to give some of your time and use your talent for the spiritual renewal of yourself and your fellow-parishioners. Thank you very much!

Sincerely,

Pastor

Encl.

Bulletin Insert

Today, the countdown of our Time and Talent Program begins. Next weekend, you will be asked to make a commitment of your Time and Talent to one of the lay ministries of our parish. A lot of preparation has taken place. Now you are ready to make your commitment.

St. Peter in his First Letter writes, "Each one of you has received a special grace, so like good stewards responsible for all these different graces of God, put yourselves at the service of others" (4:10).

As ministers, we begin to realize that we are indeed trustees and managers of all God's gifts which are to be used in service to one another.

As ministers, our Christian life today must transform us into a holy people, a people set apart who are no longer receivers but givers of their Time and Talent.

As ministers, we become aware that sharing responsibility in ministry is our "right and duty."

Pray that the Holy Spirit will enlighten each of us to be God's faithful steward.

PLEASE PRINT

FAMILY LAST NAME ONLY

ADDRESS | PHONE NO.

CITY | ZIP CODE | HOME — OWN | RENT

St. Anthony Parish
DIOCESE OF STEUBENVILLE
CENSUS AND TALENT SURVEY

DATE

HUSBAND (OR SINGLE / WIDOWED MALE)

FIRST NAME	MIDDLE	DATE OF BIRTH		
		MO.	DAY	YEAR

EDUCATION — LIST NO. OF YEARS | SPECIFY DEGREE

GRADE SCHOOL	HIGH SCHOOL	COLLEGE	

RELIGION	BAPTIZED		CONFIRMED	
	YES	NO	YES	NO

MARITAL STATUS → MARRIED | SEPARATED | WIDOWED | SINGLE
(PLEASE CHECK)

MARRIED BY A PRIEST		ATTENDS MASS			EASTER DUTY	
YES	NO	FREQUENTLY	OCCA.	SELDOM	YES	NO

PARISH REGISTERED | PARISH ATTENDS

EMPLOYED BY: | EMPLOYER'S PH. NO. | TYPE OF WORK

LIST SPECIAL SKILLS (PLUMBER, ACCOUNTANT, ETC.)

WIFE (OR SINGLE / WIDOWED FEMALE)

FIRST NAME	MIDDLE	DATE OF BIRTH		
		MO.	DAY	YEAR

EDUCATION — LIST NO. OF YEARS | SPECIFY DEGREE

GRADE SCHOOL	HIGH SCHOOL	COLLEGE	

RELIGION	BAPTIZED		CONFIRMED	
	YES	NO	YES	NO

MARITAL STATUS → MARRIED | SEPARATED | WIDOWED | SINGLE
(PLEASE CHECK)

MARRIED BY A PRIEST		ATTENDS MASS			EASTER DUTY	
YES	NO	FREQUENTLY	OCCA.	SELDOM	YES	NO

PARISH REGISTERED | PARISH ATTENDS

EMPLOYED BY: | EMPLOYER'S PH. NO. | TYPE OF WORK

LIST SPECIAL SKILLS (NURSE, TYPIST, TEACHER, ETC.)

CHILDREN

FIRST NAME	MIDDLE	DATE & YEAR OF BIRTH	BAPTIZED		FIRST COMMUNION		CONFIRMED		SCHOOL OR EMPLOYED	ATTENDS CCD	
			YES	NO	YES	NO	YES	NO		YES	NO

PLEASE CHECK

1. If you have pre-school children, do you intend sending them to parish school? ☐ Yes ☐ No

2. If you are NOT now a member of the parish WOMEN'S organization, would you like to join? ☐ Yes ☐ No

3. If the special skill you have (shown above) can be used by your parish, would you be willing to help out occasionally? ☐ Yes ☐ No

4. Does getting to Mass present a problem for any member of the family? i.e., transportation, illness, no one to stay with children, etc.) EXPLAIN: ☐ Yes ☐ No

5. What improvement would you like to see in parish?

REMARKS:

PLEASE COMPLETE REVERSE SIDE

FAMILY LAST NAME	HUSBAND'S FIRST NAME	WIFE'S FIRST NAME	ADDRESS	PHONE, NO.

"As a member of my Parish Family and aware of my stewardship and responsibility as a Christian, I want to give of myself ... of my time and ability, as well as a worthy Sunday offering ... to show Christ by actions, and not just words, that I love Him and am grateful for His many favors."

PLEASE CHECK (✔) YOUR INTEREST IN APPROPRIATE LOCATION

(Columns: HUSBAND, WIFE, CHILD (NAME), CHILD (NAME))

EDUCATION COMMISSION

HUSBAND	WIFE	CHILD (NAME)	CHILD (NAME)	
				Serve on the Education Commission
				Interested in;
				Adult Discussion Groups
				Basic instructions in our faith
				Learning more about parents role
				Marriage preparation instruction
				Prayer groups
				Retreats
				Cursillo
				Community centered parish
				Subst. Teacher (School or CCD)
				School Office Help
				Supervise Playground
				Help form parish Library
				Help in CCD Program
				Help in Pre-school Program
				CCD Office Help

SOCIAL ACTION & COM. AFFAIRS COMMISSION

HUSBAND	WIFE	CHILD (NAME)	CHILD (NAME)	
				Serve on the commission
				Participate in and plan community affairs
				Visit the sick and elderly
				Welcome new parishoners
				Will Baby Sit
				Drive People to Mass
				Help the Poor
				Willing to help on youth activities

FINANCIAL COMMISSION

HUSBAND	WIFE	CHILD (NAME)	CHILD (NAME)	
				Count collections
				Help with fund raising activities
				Help plan budget
				Help with financial report

PROPERTY COMMISSION

HUSBAND	WIFE	CHILD (NAME)	CHILD (NAME)	
				Help with repairs
				Plan for future needs of Parish

PLEASE CHECK (✔) YOUR INTERESTS IN APPROPRIATE LOCATION

(Columns: HUSBAND, WIFE, CHILD (NAME), CHILD (NAME))

LITURGICAL COMMISSION

HUSBAND		Serve	WIFE	CHILD (NAME)	CHILD (NAME)
	Serve on Liturigical Commission				
	Serve Mass				
	Serve as Lector				
	Serve as Usher				
	Sing in Choir				
	Play Organ				
	Play Guitars				
	Make Banners				
	Help decorate Church				
	Planning Liturgies (Sundays)				
	Baptisms				
	First Communion				
	Confirmations				
	May Processions				

RECREATION COMMISSION

HUSBAND		WIFE	CHILD (NAME)	CHILD (NAME)
	Serve on Recreation Committee			
	Work on Social Events			
	Picnics			
	Dances			
	Other			
	Assisting grade school sports programs			
	Scouting Program			
	Friendship Club			
	Interested in Encounters for Youth			

PERSONNEL COMMISSION

HUSBAND		WIFE	CHILD (NAME)	CHILD (NAME)
	Office work for the parish			
	Mailing and telephoning			
	Work on Parish Newsletter			

ECUMENISM COMMISSION

HUSBAND		WIFE	CHILD (NAME)	CHILD (NAME)
	Plan prayer gatherings of all faiths			
	Work in the clothes closets			
	Work on FISH			

Christian Community
Our Personal Commitment of Talents

PROCEDURES:

1. Gather the family or friends in prayer. You might read Matthew 25:14–30, reflect in silence, and share its meaning with one another.

2. Read each Area of Mission and share its meaning with one another.

3. Place first name or initial after your "Commitments." Please understand that every "Commitment" may be withdrawn if it's not what you thought it would be, so please "check it" even if it's just to learn more about it.

4. Have each member of the family sign the Commitment.

5. Either have a member of the family present the Commitment at Mass on Sunday, drop in the Sunday basket, or mail to rectory.

To fulfill the MISSION OF EVANGELIZATION, whereby we will seek to deepen our faith in the good news of Jesus Christ, and bring it to those who do not believe, I (we) make the commitment to:

A. Serve on the Evangelization Committee which sponsors a "Speaker's Night" for Inter-faith married couples; "Evening of Renewal" for recent Converts; "Good News" Sunday; and Bible Reading Week._____

B. Participate in "Bible Sharing Groups."_____

To fulfill the MISSION OF EDUCATION, whereby all members may have an opportunity to foster a personal faith through knowledge of the word of God, I (we) make the commitment to:

A. Assist Executive Committee in promoting the values of Christian Education._____

B. Assist in the Christian Education of our children as a teacher of religion (teacher training program available) in Pre-School Sunday Program _____, CCD 1st Grade Home Program _____, CCD 2nd through 6th Grade Sunday Program _____, CCD 7th and 8th Grade Home Program _____, CCD 9th through 12th Grade monthly Sunday Program _____.

C. Serve on an adult-education program committee (presently forming a "Respect Life" program) _____.

To fulfill the MISSION OF PASTORAL MINISTRY, whereby all members will work together in various lay and priestly ministries to make Christ more present, I (we) make the commitment to:

A. Serve on Committee to study the needs, review present programs, and recommend programs for the spiritual enrichment of our parish. _____

B. Serve on your Area Steering Committee which plans and executes Area activities. _____

C. Serve as Cluster "P-R" person to keep Cluster (6 to 10 families) informed and invite to Area activities. _____

D. Assist your Area Steering Committee to set up for 3 Area Masses. _____

E. Represent and plan programs among our young adults, single and married, ages 19 to 35. _____

F. Serve as adult advisor for our Parish Teen Council. _____

G. Assist as typist or contact person for our monthly newsletter. _____

To fulfill the MISSION OF LITURGY, whereby our sense of worship in Communion with God and one another may be deepened and enriched, I (we) make the commitment to:

A. Membership on our Liturgical Committee which plans any of our Liturgies. _____

B. Service at our Liturgies as: Lector _____, Usher _____, Guitarist _____, Adult Choir _____, Extraordinary Minister _____, Banner-maker _____, Cantor _____, Organist _____, Other Instrument _____, _____, Folk Choir _____, Altar Boy (6th Grade) _____, Area phone caller for our Sunday Offertory Procession Gift-Bearers _____.

To fulfill the MISSION OF SOCIAL JUSTICE AND SOCIAL WELFARE, whereby we can take an active part in helping all persons realize their human dignity as children of God, I (we) make the commitment to:

A. Serve on our Parish Social Action Committee. _____

B. Assist our Christian Support group in giving support to people who are alone or are going through some kind of upheaval in their lives. _____

C. Assist our Funeral Committee in providing luncheons for the bereaved.

D. Be "on call" to take food to needy families one day every other week. _____

E. Assist in the distribution of furniture _____ or clothing _____ in our Parish banks.

F. Represent our parish at city, county, and governmental meetings. _____

To fulfill the MISSION OF ECUMENISM, whereby we can share our faith and receive spiritual insights from people of other religious denominations, I (we) make the commitment to:

A. Serve on our Parish Ecumenical Committee. _____

B. Participate in Inter-Faith Discussion groups. _____

C. Become an active member of Church Women United. _____

To fulfill the MISSION OF SUPPORTIVE MINISTRIES, whereby we can experience a Christian community with Christ as the center of our parish by the generous giving of our time and talent, I (we) make a commitment to:

A. Serve on our Parish Finance Committee. _____

B. Assist in Bingo as kitchen help _____, "on the floor" help _____, or as Bingo "caller." _____

Being unable to participate actively in any of the above areas, I (we) hereby promise to support the other members of my parish community by my prayers and/or personal giving of my time for other areas of involvement not listed above. _____

WE, the family of _____ residing at _____ zip _____ phone _____ area no. _____ (no. given at upper right side of address), members of _____ Christian community, have made this commitment of our talents for the period of _____ through _____, on this day of _____ in the month of _____, 19_____, in the name of the Father, the Son, and the Holy Spirit.

Adult: _____

Adult: _____

Children, and all other parishioners:

_____

_____

_____

_____

_____

_____

_____

As a member of my parish and aware of my responsibility as a Christian, I want to give of myself and of my time and talent, as well as share in the building up of our parish family. I have indicated the areas where I can be of service.

Time and Talent Survey

Name _____ Address _____
Occupation _____ Telephone_____ Age _____
(optional)

SPIRITUAL LIFE AND LITURGY COMMISSION MEMBER

_____ Commission member   _____ Sacristy work (cleaning, decorating)
_____ Sing in the choir   _____ Serve as Communion distributor
_____ Serve as usher   _____ Attend days of recollection
_____ Serve as lector   _____ Attend retreat
_____ Be server at Liturgy   _____ Participate in prayer group
_____ Organist
_____ Musician

CHRISTIAN EDUCATION COMMISSION MEMBER

_____ Commission member   _____ School board
_____ Participate in Bible study   _____ High school board
_____ C.C.D. teacher _____ Age level _____ Home/school
_____ Adult education coordinator   _____ School athletics
_____ Attend adult education programs _____ Cheerleaders
                                           _____ Coach

_____
         Topic Suggestions
_____
         Topic Suggestions
_____ Work with youth program
_____ Volunteer work in the school
_____ Volunteer with Sunday C.C.D. pro-
            gram

CHRISTIAN SERVICE COMMISSION

_____ Commission member
_____ Work with St. Vincent de Paul
_____ Visit the sick
_____ Visit the elderly
_____ Hospital visitation
_____ Rest home visitation

FAMILY LIFE COMMISSION MEMBER

_____ Men's club/couples' club
_____ Parish dances
_____ Parish sporting events
_____ Golf club
_____ Marriage Encounter
_____ Family retreat
_____ Divorced Catholic program
_____ Cursillo
_____ Social youth group
_____ Nursery volunteer

COMMUNICATIONS COMMISSION MEMBER

_____ Commission member
_____ Type parish newsletter
_____ Parish calendar
_____ Welcoming commission
_____ Follow-up visits to newcomers

_____ Compile and edit newsletter
_____ Sunday morning coffee
_____ Keep updated parish directory
_____ Organize phone chain
_____ Be part of phone chain

ADMINISTRATION COMMISSION MEMBER

_____ Commission member
_____ Keep parish records
_____ Do bookkeeping and/or banking
_____ Budget preparation and assist with budgets of local groups
_____ Audit books
_____ Do minor carpentry repairs
_____ Do minor electrical repairs

_____ Do minor painting
_____ Furnish trucking service
_____ Do landscaping, lawn work
_____ Other fund raising

_____ Festival commission
_____ Festival worker
_____ D.D.F. worker

Time and Talent Offering

Name _____ Phone_____

I have checked below the areas of service that I am or would like to be involved in this year as my contribution to our parish community.

WORSHIP

_____ Art Work	_____ Sacristan
_____ Clean Church	_____ Sewing
_____ Lector	_____ Usher
_____ Server	_____ Adult Choir
_____ Songleader	_____ Children's Choir
_____ Organist	_____ Folk Group

AID TO PARISH

_____ Ecumenical Committee
_____ Finance and Properties
_____ Social Committee
_____ Communications/Publicity
_____ Telephone Contact
_____ Typing
_____ Library Cataloguing
_____ Help fold, staple occasional parish publications

OTHER TIME AND TALENT OFFERING

1)_____

_____

2)_____

_____

FORMATION

Education Committee:

_____ a) Elementary	_____ c) Adult
_____ b) High School	_____ d) Social Concerns

_____ Study Groups
_____ Teaching
_____ Teacher Substitute

AID TO PERSONS

_____ Catholic Community Services
_____ Neighborhood Center
_____ Mental Health Society Visitor:
    Visitor:
_____ a) Hospital
_____ b) Nursing Homes
_____ c) Shut-ins, Sick
    Transportation to:

_____ a) Nursing Homes	_____ d) Religion Classes
_____ b) Shut-ins	_____ e) Doctor
_____ c) Mass on weekends	_____ f) Store

_____ Willing to do minor household repairs for the elderly
_____ Cook for the sick
_____ Prepare food baskets when needed
_____ Cut grass, rake leaves, trim shrubs for those who cannot

Time and Talent Survey

Name _____ Address _____
Occupation _____ Phone _____ Age _____
                                                                    (optional)

    As a member of my parish and aware of my responsibility as a Christian, I want to give of myself and of my time and talent as well as share in the building of our parish family. I have indicated the areas I can be of service.

I. SPIRITUAL LIFE AND LITURGY COMMITTEE

_____ Committee Member
_____ Serve as Usher
_____ Serve as Lector
_____ Be Server at Liturgy
_____ Organist
_____ Musician
_____ Sacristy Work (cleaning, decorating)
_____ Participate in Prayer Group
_____ Offertory Gift Bearer

_____ Lay Distributor
_____ Attend Days of Recollection
_____ Attend Retreat
_____ Liturgy Planning
_____ Hymn Leader
_____ Folk Group Member
_____ All Night Adoration
_____ May Crowning

II. CHRISTIAN EDUCATION COMMITTEE

_____ Committee Member

_____ Participate in Bible Study
_____ C.C.D. Teacher _____ Age Level
_____ Attend Adult Education Program
Topic Suggestions _____

_____ Catholic Elementary or High School Boards
_____ Sacramental Preparation
_____ Marriage Instruction
_____ Adult Education
_____ Volunteer with Sunday C.C.D. Program (Pre-School)

III. SOCIAL CONCERNS COMMITTEE

_____ Committee Member
_____ Work with St. Vincent de Paul
_____ Visit the Sick
_____ Hospital Visitation
_____ Rest Home Visitation
_____ Visit the Elderly

_____ Senior Citizens Club
_____ Bereavement Concerns
_____ Transportation for Elderly
_____ Provide Home in Emergency
_____ First Friday Communion Calls

IV. FAMILY AND PARISH LIFE COMMITTEE

_____ Men's Club/Women's Club
_____ Parish Dances
_____ Golf League
_____ Marriage Encounter
_____ Family Retreat
_____ Single Again Program
_____ Welcome Committee
_____ Pre Cana program
_____ Pot Luck Dinners

_____ Christmas Pot Luck
_____ Festival
_____ Couples' Club
_____ First Sunday Coffee & Doughnuts
_____ Help Plan Parish Events
_____ Boy Scouts
_____ Parish Sporting Events
_____ Cursillo
_____ Special Youth Program

V. ADMINISTRATION COMMITTEE

_____ Committee Member	_____ Furnish Trucking Service
_____ Keep Parish Records	_____ Do Landscaping, Lawn Work
_____ Financial Planning & Review	_____ Other Fund Raising
_____ Do Minor Carpentry Repairs	_____ Festival Commission
_____ Do Minor Electrical Repairs	_____ Festival Worker
_____ Typing	_____ Bishop's Annual Appeal
_____ Help with Newsletter	_____ Census Work
_____ Minor Plumbing Work	_____ Telephone Contact
_____ Snow Removal	_____ Help Staple
_____ Do Minor Painting	_____ Census
	_____ Bulletin

The Time/Talent Survey Leadership Identification Process

STEP 1

The pastor should assemble a group of three to five persons who meet the following criteria.

A. They each have a knowledge of the parish and its Vision.

B. They have a basic understanding of the type of person who can work well in leadership within the parish.

C. They should recognize they are offering input to the pastor and are not the final decision makers.

D. Each person must be the type who will not discuss the process or its outcome with anyone.

E. They have exemplified a keen awareness of the value of prayer in Christian life.

STEP 2

The pastor should review all job descriptions with the group and then take each job description separately through the next steps.

STEP 3

The pastor should distribute the list of names gathered from the Time/Talent Survey as a basis for selection of names for leadership. This does not preclude the possibility of surfacing names not on the list. (Having a parish roster on hand is a must.)

STEP 4

The pastor should ask the individuals to spend two to three minutes individually listing their "first reaction" names of the "right" persons for the job in rank order, giving at least three choices.

STEP 5

The pastor should then make a full list of all individuals suggested, asking the group not to react until all names are posted.

STEP 6

With the entire list clearly visible, the pastor should ask each group member to share with the group his or her reasons for suggesting each name.

STEP 7

Each person should then reconsider the choices and rank order his or her top three choices privately on an index card. The pastor should collect the card from each so that he can indicate on the aggregate list the frequency of first, second and third choices for each person.

STEP 8

This process should be repeated for each job, even though some parishioners will be chosen for more than one position. One way to avoid too much duplication is to eliminate the top choice for each ministry from being top choice in any other.

STEP 9

A period of prayer should be incorporated, providing the base and wellspring for the ministerial growth of individual and parish.

Obviously, this group may have to meet more than once to consider more than two or three ministries. The participants need to bear in mind that the information is confidential and that the pastor must have the final decision.

All who volunteered on the Time and Talent Survey are contacted as quickly as possible to express thanks and assurance that their offer is being accepted.

Once the volunteer ministries are on the job, the lists of others willing to help are shared with them as well as any committee or organization for which services have been offered.

Building a Prospect List

Upon completion of a Time and Talent Survey, the parish will have a list of potential volunteers. However, for two reasons, it may be necessary to develop a list of volunteers without the assistance of a survey. They are:

1. A parish is just beginning to use volunteer leadership and cannot do an effective Time and Talent Survey until the core group is on-board, or

2. The parish completed a Time and Talent Survey and no one volunteered for some of the ministries. Another use would be for core group or ministry leaders to develop resource lists of volunteers.

In each case, the following process can be followed. First, however, a word of caution. The Prospecting Process is an *emergency* procedure. It lacks validity for ongoing use because it does not permit all in the parish to participate in *offering* their service. Do not use this process more than once.

The Process

STEP 1

The pastor should assemble a group of three to five persons who meet the following criteria:

A. They together have a substantial knowledge of a broad cross section of the parishioners.

B. They have a basic understanding of the type of person that can work well within the parish community.

C. The group should be able to deal with the fact that they are offering input to the pastor and are not the final decision makers.

D. Each person must be the type who will not discuss the process or its outcome with anyone.

E. Each has exemplified a keen awareness of the value of prayer in the Christian life.

STEP 2

The pastor should review all job descriptions with the group and then take each job description separately through the next steps.

STEP 3

The pastor should ask the individuals to spend two to three minutes individually listing their "first reaction" names of the "right" persons for the job in rank order. Give at least three choices.

NOTE

Having a parish roster on hand is a must.

STEP 4

The pastor should then make a full list of all individuals suggested, asking the group not to react until all names are posted.

STEP 5

With the entire list clearly visible, the pastor should ask each group member to share with the group his or her reasons for suggesting each name.

STEP 6

Each person should then reconsider the choices and rank order his or her top three choices privately on an index card. The pastor should collect the card from each so that he can indicate on the aggregate list the frequency of first, second and third choices for each person.

STEP 7

The process should be repeated for each job, even though some parishioners will be chosen for more than one position. One way to avoid too much duplication is to eliminate the top choice for each ministry from being top choice in any others.

STEP 8

A period of prayer should be incorporated, providing the base and wellspring for the ministerial growth of individual and parish.

Obviously, this group may have to meet more than once to consider more than two or three ministries. They must be cautioned to discuss the information with no one, since the pastor must have the ability to make final choices without offending other candidates.

Whichever system is used to arrive at the final list of potential volunteer ministers, the pastor should keep a record of the names of the top prospects in the file of each ministry. In the event the person finally chosen does not work out or must resign, retention of such a list will be helpful in the selection of a successor.

III. Ministry Directory

This section outlines job descriptions for selected parish ministries. In order to be of value the job descriptions need to be tailored to the local situation, adding or deleting whatever responsibilities are appropriate to the parish community.

Job Title: Minister of Temporalities

ON THE JOB SUPERVISOR
Pastor

OBJECTIVE
To assure proper utilization of parish resources, development, and monitoring of budget and budget process, parish support and the maintenance of parish facilities.

RESPONSIBILITIES
To establish a working relationship with staff, parish council, committees and organizations.

PHYSICAL PLANT
1. Responsible for maintenance of existing buildings and planning for any additional needed buildings or properties.

2. A practical knowledge of what maintenance can be handled in house and what needs to be contracted.

3. A knowledge of diocesan and local community resources.

FINANCES
1. Responsible for the development of the annual budget for parish life and the monitoring of that budget in light of faith Vision of the parish.

2. Responsible for the development of an adequate parish offertory program.

3. Responsible for any special drives and/or appeals necessary for the diocesan and/or parish upkeep.

4. To review and approve all banking arrangements, capital expenses and long term contracts.

QUALIFICATIONS
1. A practical knowledge of the workings of physical facilities.

2. A good understanding of contracts in the parish and community for work which must be bid.

3. The ability to look to the future of buildings and properties and plan for effective and efficient usage.

4. Knowledge of finances.

5. Able to relate well with people.

6. A desire to be involved in volunteer ministry.

7. Acceptance and willingness to incorporate parish Vision in ministry.

TRAINING AND PREPARATION FOR THE JOB
1. A good business experience.

2. Orientation to the diocesan and parish process and procedures related to both finance and properties.

3. Access to all books and procedures.

4. Specific training as necessary for personal development.

EVALUATION
Through standard performance appraisal system

COMMITMENT
A 2–3 year commitment. This task requires about 6–8 hours weekly.

During the period of time that quarterly reports are to be completed at least 25 hours will be required for one week. At the end of the year report time at least 60 hours will be required.

Job Title: Coordinator of Religious Education

ON THE JOB SUPERVISOR
Pastor

OBJECTIVE
To plan, implement, and staff religious education programs in the parish which will meet the needs of parishioners at all levels.

RESPONSIBILITIES
General: To establish relationship with staff, parish council, organizations and committees.

1. To coordinate elementary and secondary religious education programs.

2. To recruit and train teachers and aides for all programs.

3. To assure ample materials and resources for all programs.

4. To coordinate sacramental preparation for the parish.

5. To recruit team members for the sacramental preparation program.

6. To insure training and educational materials for all programs.

7. To provide catechumenate instructions.

8. To provide an adult education program.

QUALIFICATIONS
1. Knowledge of religious education, theology—or related fields as directed by the diocese.

2. Knowledge of the *National Catechetical Directory.*

3. Ability to relate to students and teachers.

4. Organizational, management and communications skills.

5. Able to teach and to supervise.

6. Strong faith that translates into a Catholic life-style.

7. Recognition of the theology of the pastor and parish and the ability to develop religious education programs to support and promote growth in that reality.

8. Ability to accept and implement parish Vision.

TRAINING
The pastor should provide for training at parish or diocesan level.

EVALUATION
Through standard performance appraisal system.

COMMITMENT
Two years. Amount of time each week will depend upon the number of classes scheduled each day and the size of enrollment.

Job Title: Minister of Social, Recreational and Ecumenical Concerns

ON THE JOB SUPERVISOR
Pastor

OBJECTIVE
To coordinate activities and programs of a parish nature for both direct service and education in social justice and ecumenical involvement as well as recreational activities.

RESPONSIBILITIES
General: To establish a working relationship with staff, parish council, committees, and organizations.

1. To offer advocacy for the disadvantaged: unemployed, poor, uneducated, handicapped, etc.

2. To offer support and direction for the Golden Age Club, etc.

3. To coordinate assistance and service to bereaved families and homes.

4. To encourage meetings of priest and ministers at ministerial society.

5. To coordinate events that will bring together people of different faiths.

6. To respond to crisis situations.

7. To coordinate events of a recreational nature for parishioners.

QUALIFICATIONS

1. Desire to work within the parish.

2. Ability to motivate and stimulate parish interest in social ministry.

3. Ability to listen and support without becoming overly involved.

4. Ability to delegate and to coordinate.

5. Organizational skills and communication skills.

6. Compassion and patience.

7. Acceptance of and willingness to implement parish Vision.

TRAINING

The pastor should provide training opportunities in the community and at the diocesan level to assist in development of particular skills.

EVALUATION

Through standard performance appraisal system.

COMMITMENT

Two years would be ideal, with a weekly commitment of 8–10 hours as needs demand. This is a ministry where emergencies may arise and the minister needs to be able to respond directly or through delegation.

Job Title: Youth Minister

ON THE JOB SUPERVISOR

Pastor

OBJECTIVE

To foster the personal and spiritual growth of each young person. To draw young people to responsible participation in the life, mission and work of the faith community.

RESPONSIBILITIES

General: To establish a working relationship with staff, parish council, committees and organizations.

1. Coordinate all youth ministry programming.

2. Identify the youth of the parish and their religious and moral needs.

3. To recruit and coordinate adults in the parish who are interested in and have the ability to communicate and work with youth.

4. To establish and coordinate multifaceted programs and experiences to reach youth and their spiritual needs.

5. Cooperate with diocesan efforts in youth ministry.

6. Work in cooperation with local schools and churches and be knowledgeable of the social activities of the youth.

7. Challenge the parish youth to determine how they can best contribute their talents to the parish community.

8. Cooperate with other staff in developing and implementing parish programs.

9. Work with parents of adolescents in helping them recognize and adjust to this period of transition in the lives of their sons and/or daughters.

10. Present an annual evaluation of parish youth ministry to pastor, staff and council.

QUALIFICATIONS

1. Knowledge of and ability to manage, organize and communicate.

2. Willing to exemplify a personal commitment to church.

3. Ability to establish total spiritual experiences as well as social activities for youth.

4. Ability to motivate and stimulate the youth to identify and participate in the life of the parish.

5. Ability to relate to various socio-economic and ethnic groups.

6. Willing to work with youth and parents.

7. Acceptance of and willingness to implement parish Vision.

TRAINING

Training in religious education, counseling, social work and related fields should be provided through diocesan offices.

EVALUATION
Through standard performance appraisal system.

COMMITMENT
Two years. At least 8–10 hours a week with evenings on call. Frequent weekend activities.

Job Title: Spiritual Life Minister

ON THE JOB SUPERVISOR
Pastor

OBJECTIVE
To provide a variety of activities that support and extend the spiritual life of the parish and faith community.

RESPONSIBILITIES
General: To establish working relationship with staff, parish council, committees and organizations.

1. Further development of spiritual growth programs in the parish (continuance, follow-up and evolution to other programs).

2. The development of the above programs adequate to all ages in parish life.

3. Develop a parish library, prayer network, etc.

QUALIFICATIONS
1. Strong moral character, hopefully with leadership training and a history of participation in spiritual growth.

2. Willingness to grow in the spiritual life by attendance at retreats, workshops on spiritual growth, study and prayer groups.

3. Acceptance of and willingness to implement parish Vision.

TRAINING AND PREPARATION
Training for this ministry will be determined by the minister and pastor as decisions on program are made and needs of the minister become obvious.

EVALUATION
Through standard performance appraisal system.

COMMITMENT
Two years would be ideal with at least two to three days a week spread over times when parishioners are available. It may be one full day and several evenings.

Job Title: Liturgy Coordination Minister

ON THE JOB SUPERVISOR
Pastor

OBJECTIVE
To provide adequate education, information and experience in the liturgical and sacramental life of the parish faith community.

RESPONSIBILITIES
1. To establish working relationship with staff, parish council, committees and organizations.

2. To call together and train groups of people to prepare and carry through Sunday liturgies and special celebrations of liturgical nature.

3. To provide recruitment, training, coordination of liturgical ministers (cantors, lectors, servers, eucharistic ministers and greeters).

4. To provide for total music ministry.

5. To educate parishioners to understand and actively participate in the liturgy.

6. To evaluate the liturgical life and programs of the parish.

7. To arrange for parishioners' input to homily preparation.

8. To provide ongoing education for the liturgy committee.

QUALIFICATIONS
1. Appreciation of the worship of the church.

2. Sensitivity to the current growth of the parish in the life of liturgy.

3. Willingness to learn about Vatican II implications and liturgy.

4. Ability to work with teams.

5. Organizational skills.

6. Acceptance of and willingness to incorporate parish Vision.

TRAINING AND PREPARATION FOR THE JOB

Training will be conducted through materials and guidance at the parish and diocesan level. Workshops available in and beyond the diocese are also suggested, along with any appropriate training for the specific areas in which the minister is working.

EVALUATION

Through standard performance appraisal system.

COMMITMENT

Two to three years. This is a responsibility that would require at least 8–10 hours a week and evenings. Each weekend might require a considerable amount of time until other volunteers are able to assume some of the on-site tasks.

Major feast days will require additional time depending on the level of assistance the minister has developed.

Job Title: Support Minister

ON THE JOB SUPERVISOR

Pastor

OBJECTIVE

To provide necessary clerical and supportive assistance to parish staff in areas of clerical and financial assistance.

RESPONSIBILITIES

General: To establish working relationship with staff, parish council, committees, and organizations as needed.

1. Understands the total parish ministry, the Vision and the relationship to other parishes and the diocese.

2. Serves as telephone and office receptionist.

3. Maintains filing system: general office file, parish membership file, sacramental file, etc.

4. Prepares and coordinates calendar for parish including meeting room reservations.

5. Prepares weekly bulletin and possibly monthly newsletter.

6. Types correspondence as necessary.

7. Counts money and posts receipts.

8. Duplicates materials as necessary.

9. Prepares purchase orders.

10. Prepares bills for payment, writes checks, mail.

11. Prepares bank deposits and other payments.

12. Does bookkeeping.

13. Prepares payroll.

14. Attends staff meetings as needed and prayer sessions.

15. Assumes other responsibilities enumerated by the pastor.

QUALIFICATIONS

1. General business background and experience depending on recentness of employment.

2. Skills, such as typing, shorthand or filing, general math, bookkeeping or accounting.

3. Ability to project in person and on the telephone the compassion and concern of the parish staff.

4. Ability to maintain parish confidentiality.

TRAINING

Training will be of an enrichment nature along with the assistance of diocesan personnel as appropriate and should be provided under the direction of the pastor.

EVALUATION

Through standard performance appraisal system.

COMMITMENT

Two to three years with 8–10 hours per week.

Performance Appraisal Process

Performance appraisal provides the opportunity for a volunteer minister and pastor to discuss and evaluate the progress of the ministry.

The process we have outlined first explains the purpose of a performance appraisal and clearly demonstrates that the system is not designed to concentrate on the effectiveness of the person but on the development of the ministry. It is true that the personality of any minister may create problems within a program but this is the exception. If this should occur and it becomes necessary to dismiss a minister the pastor should follow the process suggested in the section "Exit Interviews."

The standard performance appraisal process should be carefully discussed with the prospective volunteer minister prior to finalizing the agreement.

Two weeks prior to a review the pastor should give the forms to the volunteer and review the procedure once again.

At this time the pastor should indicate the date, time and place of the review. During the two weeks prior to the interview the pastor and volunteer should complete the forms and those things indicated in the following under the section "Preparing for the Review."

The session itself should begin with a simple review of purpose and then discussion of the accomplishments and disappointments the minister has experienced over a given period of time (one year, a quarter, etc.).

The minister is then asked to discuss the specific responsibilities of the job description and describe the implementation of those tasks to date.

The Appraisal form includes a segment entitled "Objective." Each ministry volunteer is asked to specify a limited number of concerns that he or she feels are those areas in which he or she needs to concentrate energy and effort in the coming months. Guidelines as to what is to be included are stated on the form.

The concluding aspect of the review offers the volunteer an opportunity to make any comments or observations he or she feels important to his or her ministry.

The pastor should allow the volunteer ample time to discuss each area, listening, offering suggestions and direction. It is sometimes the pastor's responsibility to make the volunteer aware of areas in which he or she has not demonstrated his or her ability to be effective. This can be in ministry related skills or in human relations skills. This discussion should be dealt with honestly, sincerely and compassionately. It is important that the volunteer understand what behavior or skill is expect-ed and/or is not expected and how to rectify the situation. These are usually added to the objectives.

At the end of the interview both pastor and volunteer minister sign the form. A copy is kept on file in the office and the volunteer is given a copy.

Annually, it is advisable for the pastor to give a personnel report to the council and/or staff. This report simply states those areas where there has been significant growth and specific needs he and the volunteer ministers have identified. This system should also be used by the volunteer ministers with each of the people reporting to them and so on down the line.

Performance Appraisal System

Purpose of Performance Appraisal

1. A gnneral summary of the past period results versus previously agreed upon targets and/or performance standards.

2. A review of progress on objectives.

3. A discussion of behavior which affects the attainment of desired results.

4. Plans to alleviate problems.

5. Discussion of personal development.

Preparing for the Review

1. Pastor's responsibility

a. Review general background information
b. Review in-depth the immediate past
—Performance against job description
—Mutually agreed upon objectives
—Aspects needing improvement
c. Complete review form

2. Volunteer's responsibility

a. List of accomplishments and disappointments
b. Review strengths and weaknesses
c. Steps to improve performance
d. Complete form

The Review

1. Set specific date/length of session/place and schedule a meeting at least two weeks in advance to allow for preparation.

2. At the meeting:

a. Review the purpose of the appraisal.
b. Look at the accomplishments and disappointments.
c. Review performance against job description.
d. Review any progress against objective previously set.
e. Determine areas, two or three, to be concentrated on and how to develop them.
f. Volunteer's input.

3. A signed copy of the review should be filed with the pastor and a copy given to the volunteer.

Follow-up

A periodic report of progress of volunteer ministries should be given by the pastor to the staff and council in general and directional terms.

Frequency

The general rule is that every volunteer minister should be reviewed annually. In the event there is cause to do so more frequently we recommend that a quarterly review is an effective means to monitor more closely the progress an individual is making.

Quarterly reviews might certainly be in order the first year.

Resources for Ministers

In each area of ministry in a parish there is a person or department at the diocesan level who can serve as a resource for materials, training and information. The parish volunteer should obtain this person's/department's name and number and set up an initial visit to determine what services and resources are available in or through the office.

E.g. Coordinator of Religious Education in a parish should contact the Office of Religious Education to learn of textbooks, training sessions, audio-visual aids and many other services that may be provided to parishes.

Basic Resources

All parish volunteer ministers would find the following sources of great benefit:

Documents of Vatican II, Edited by Austin P. Flannery. Costello Publishing Company, Northport, N.Y. 11768.

The Publications Office, United States Catholic Conference, 1312 Massachusetts Avenue, N.W., Washington, D.C. 20005. This office provides catalogues of publications which relate to all areas of Church ministry as well as all of the bishops' statements on any given topic.

SPECIAL SUGGESTED AIDS
TO MINISTERS IN PARISHES

Area	Resources
1. Religious Education	*National Catechetical Directory: Sharing the Light of Faith,* United States Catholic Conference, 1312 Massachusetts Avenue, N.W., Washington, D.C. 20005
2. Youth Ministry	*Building a Rainbow,* United States Catholic Conference, 1312 Massachusetts Avenue, N.W., Washington, D.C. 20005
3. Liturgy	*Liturgy Committee Handbook,* Salt Lake City Liturgical Commission 333 E. South Temple, Salt Lake City, Utah 84111 *Strategies for Effective Liturgy Meetings,* Archdiocese of Detroit 305 Michigan Avenue Detroit, Michigan 48226
4. Social Concerns	*Empowerment,* Harry Fagan, published by Paulist Press *Ministry to the Hospitalized,* Gerald Niklas and Charlotte Stefancis published by Paulist Press *Aging and Ministry,* Henri Nouwen, published by Paulist Press *Abortion,* by John Powell, published by Paulist Press Bread for the World, 6411 Chillum Pl., N.W. Washington, D.C. 20012 *Renewing the Earth: Catholic Documents on Peace, Justice and Liberation,* edited by David O'Brien and Thomas Shannon, Doubleday Image Books, New York
5. Spiritual Development (Renewal)	Christ Renews His Parish St. Joseph Christian Life Center 18485 Lake Shore Boulevard Cleveland, Ohio 44119 *Renew* Paulist Press 545 Island Road Ramsey, N.J. 07446
6. Ecumenical	Ecumenical Trends Graymoor Garrison, New York 10524

Volunteer's Performance Appraisal

Name _____ Date _____
Starting Date _____

Performance Characteristics Evaluation
Commentary: Explain what has been accomplished in each area and the quality of performance.

1. _____

_____

2. _____

_____

3. _____

_____

4. _____

_____

5. _____

_____

6. _____

_____

7. _____

_____

8. _____

_____

Objectives: Select three areas for concentration of growth efforts prior to next review.
   1. State *what* is to be done.

   2. State *how* it will be accomplished.

   3. State *what* resources will assist in its accomplishment.

1. _____

_____

_____

_____

2. _____
_____
_____
_____

3. _____
_____
_____
_____

Other comments by volunteer.

_____
_____
_____

Signed_____ Signed_____
             Pastor   Volunteer

IV. Recruiting Volunteers

Selecting the Volunteer

Now that the processes of identifying the needed ministries and researching the list of potential volunteers have been completed, it is time to select the very best prospect. Since the pastor holds the ultimate responsibility for the performance of the team, he must accept the responsibility of final selection and recruiting.

The pastor should work on one ministry at a time. He should have the following available:

1. The *job description* and qualifications for the ministry.

2. A record of the past involvement of each prospect.

Item 2 is important. In the rush to recruit people, their *real* prior record is often overlooked. It is incumbent upon the pastor to review each prospect carefully. Put each name on a separate sheet and make notes by reflecting on the following questions:

1. Is it probable that the person is fully committed to the theological and ministerial direction of the parish?

2. Has the person managed parish projects in the past?

3. If so, did the person work well with other volunteers and with the pastor?

4. Is the person part of a possible negative group within the parish?

5. Does the person fully participate in all important aspects of parish life?

6. Can the person perform the job required and still fulfill his or her role at home and at work?

7. Is it possible that the person might use the ministry to escape responsibilities or problems at home or at work?

8. Based on the above answers and overall qualifications, is this individual a good choice?

Having answered all of the above questions, it will be clear that no one is available to fill any positions. In recognition of the fact that no one is perfect, we admonish the pastor that the list is only intended to provide food for thought. Some questions are more relevant than others. It is up to the pastor to provide the weighting factor for each answer and, after prayer and reflection, select the top two candidates for the ministry.

Now the pastor is ready to recruit the top candidate.

Recruiting

It must be understood that recruiting is more than asking and less than selling. When recruiting a volunteer you cannot usually gain acceptance of a position by simply asking. People are not willing to assume another major task that easily.

On the other hand, you aren't served well by selling the person on the job. Selling can often result in unwitting or deliberate deceptions on the part of the seller. When you very much want a person on the team it gets easy to promise assistance and many hours of support and training and then not deliver on those promises.

Recruiting is a process that involves planning and should be done in much the same way for each new volunteer. First, the pastor should resolve in his own mind the *real* support that will be available to the person when on board. Second, the pastor should not *hit* the person to be recruited after Mass or on the phone. Rather, he should call and arrange an appointment with the individual and his or her spouse. The time and place for the appointment should be that which is most convenient for the volunteer. Usually the meeting is best held at the prospect's home. Avoid discussion of the reason for the appointment. You may say too much about the job and run the risk of being rejected on the first contact.

When the pastor meets the prospect and spouse he should proceed as follows:

1. Discuss the Vision of the parish.

2. Discuss the role of the laity and specifically lay ministry in helping fulfill the Vision.

3. Describe the process used to arrive at the names of the individuals who will be asked to serve.

4. Give the prospect and spouse separate copies of the job description.

5. Walk them through the job description task by task.

6. Cite why you feel that the prospect is the right person.

7. Ask them to reflect prayerfully about the request for a couple of days. The pastor should join the couple in praying for guidance of the Spirit in making this important decision.

Finally, before the meeting ends, the pastor should seek agreement as to a date and time for an initial interview with the prospect at the rectory. Obviously, that appointment can be canceled if the prospect decides not to serve.

It should be made clear to the prospect that the *interview* is the point for a final decision for both the pastor and the prospect. The purpose of the recruiting meeting is to brief the prospect and spouse on the parameters of the task and establish an initial willingness to seriously consider serving.

SOME TIPS ON RECRUITING

The following items have been adapted from "Basic Tools for Recruitment." They should be reviewed before meeting with the prospective volunteer.

INVOLVING THE UNINVOLVED IN VOLUNTEER MINISTRY

1. Broaden the knowledge of parishioners about parish needs. Let people know that your parish is attempting to solve problems affecting them by recruiting volunteers.

2. Convince parishioners of the reality of the need for volunteer help.

3. Telephone recruitment is not a positive way to recruit. Since the phone is used by market research firms, sales people and bill collectors, people have developed an ease in saying "no" over the phone.

4. Show the real need you have for his or her services. Be honest. Do not glamorize or minimize the ministry.

5. Show benefits that can be derived from the effort of those helping. What does a volunteer stand to gain as a result of volunteering for the parish? Appeal to the sense of dedication and commitment.

6. Promise a good character and business reference when a volunteer does a good job for you. Stress the fact that this reference has value to a future employer.

7. Don't try to push an individual into accepting a ministry. He or she might say yes out of desperation and then leave the scene as soon as possible.

AFTER THE VOLUNTEER IS ON BOARD

8. Involve the volunteer in planning for the work to be done. The person who shuns clubs and community groups may welcome the opportunity to be the one in charge of a special part of the volunteer ministry.

9. Create an atmosphere of acceptance. Let the person know you would be happy to have him or her as part of the staff, team, etc.

10. Even the best volunteers may miss a day or two. Accept this as part of the scheme of things, but make it clear that you need them.

11. Differentiate between work and social time but remember that socializing is very important. Volunteering should be fun.[8]

V. Interviewing Processes

Interviewing

The steps required by this section are far more structured than those used in most volunteer situations. In fact, they require more detail than is usually applied to interviews of paid employees. This system has been developed to meet several needs. First, a certain level of formality in interviewing lets the volunteer know that his or her role is important and the work has to be done in a reasonably precise and timely way. Second, the supervisor (pastor) recognizes these factors and has selected the volunteer because of his or her ability to do the job. Third, although a volunteer position is, by definition, unpaid, the ground rules are not very different from a paid position relative to accountability, performance, and so on. Finally, the interview process creates a bridge from the less formal relationship of pastor/parishioner to the more formal relationship of pastor/volunteer minister.

This segment is divided into two major components—entrance interviews and exit interviews. Additionally, the exit interview portion is divided into segments dealing with voluntary and compulsory termination.

Entry Interviews

All interviews should take place in the pastor's office or some other convenient room in the rectory. The room should be absolutely private and disturbances should be limited as much as possible.

About 15 or 20 minutes before the meeting the pastor should prepare for the meeting by reviewing the appropriate sections of this manual. He should be sure to have on hand:

1. The job description.

2. The results of the process selection (why this person and not someone else?).

3. The pastor's definition of available training resources.

4. A list of the limits of the help the pastor can give.

5. A list of others who will be asked to fill major positions.

6. A copy of the volunteer Agreement Form.

The pastor proceeds with the meeting as follows:

1. Begin with a prayer.

2. Review the developments in the Church, diocese and parish that have made the involvement of laity crucial.

3. Ask the volunteer to complete a job application.

4. Review the application to be sure it is clear and to look for training, or experience, that will be helpful in the ministry.

5. Review the evaluation process to be used and the fact that the evaluation criteria are in the job description.

6. Cite the reasons why the volunteer was chosen.

7. Describe the training available and the amount of time you can assist with it.

8. Tell the volunteer how the team will function and who will be on it, and ask if he or she has any problem with the structure or the people.

9. Ask the person to serve (be prepared to end the meeting amicably if the answer is "no").

10. If the volunteer agrees to serve, explain the Agreement Form and have the individual complete it.

11. Give the volunteer some written training materials and explain them.

12. Give him or her a copy of the job description and explain the work plan and budget segment.

13. Schedule the next meeting at which the pastor and volunteer will produce a work plan and budget.

14. Close with a prayer.

Exit Interviews

Exit interviews are a must for a successful program even though some may be unpleasant. The voluntary interviews generally will be pleasant and, therefore, easy. It is crucial, however, to develop in the pastor's mind the need for compulsory exit interviews and the will to do them on a timely basis.

Voluntary Exit Interviews

This type of interview will occur for one of two reasons: either the volunteer's term is ending or the volunteer must resign for personal reasons, e.g., health, family or work related needs. The pastor should be aware of these potentialities and be sympathetic to them.

Do not try to talk a person out of resigning if he or she has valid reasons. The only exception to this rule occurs when the volunteers feel they are doing a poor job and the pastor honestly feels they are performing well. If this situation arises the pastor may wish to seek a short (30-60 day) interim period to work with a volunteer to help him or her see the level of performance more objectively.

The normal volunteer exit interview process follows:

1. Several days before the meeting the pastor should send a copy of the "Report and Evaluation of a Volunteer Ministry" to the minister. This report should be completed by the minister prior to the meeting.

2. The pastor should prepare for the meeting by reviewing the work plan, performance of the minister and the pastor's view of the answers he would give if completing the "Report and Evaluation."

3. After an opening prayer, the pastor should review the reasons for leaving with the volunteer. He should be supportive of the minister's decision.

4. Next, the pastor should ask the minister to review the evaluation form and describe in detail the comments made.

5. The minister should be asked for suggestions as to a replacement, and, hopefully, already will have begun to train one or more.

6. The pluses and minuses of each possible replacement should be reviewed.

7. In some cases—those where the person is resigning because of burn out in a particular position—the pastor may wish to discuss the person's availability for other parish duties as positions become available. The response should be kept on file in the event the person is willing to serve.

8. Again, in cases of burn out, the pastor may wish to suggest a leave of absence as opposed to a resignation. Each situation will have to be judged on a case by case basis, and the pastor must keep in mind that a person resigning for a valid reason should not be talked out of it.

9. Finally, the pastor should thank the volunteer for his or her service and ask him or her to deliver a final report to the team and/or parish council. This will allow these groups to present the volunteer with some sort of official recognition of service.

Compulsory Termination Interview

The fact of this type of interview occurring should come as no surprise to the volunteer minister. It should occur as part of the process of continuing evaluation. Prior meetings will most often have set the scene for this final meeting.

In contrast with the other interviews, this interview must proceed on a definite schedule. This is not the time for counseling. The service of the individual must be terminated with compassion and, most often, that is best enhanced by a well-structured agenda and fast-paced meeting.

To prepare the pastor should:

1. Review the job description.

2. Review past evaluation meeting documentation.

3. Anticipate possible reaction by the minister and the pastor's reaction to him or her.

The agenda should proceed as follows:

1. An opening prayer.

2. A review by the pastor of past evaluation sessions (10 minutes).

3. Comment by the pastor as to the lack of improvement in the problem areas (5 minutes).

4. Time for the volunteer to respond (5 minutes).

5. The pastor must then ask for the individual's resignation.

6. Quickly end the meeting and, if appropriate, suggest a time for a counseling session if the cause for termination is related to personal problems that could be helped by counseling.

NOTE 1

If the termination meeting proceeds productively and is not negative at its conclusion, it is not inappropriate to ask the minister to complete an evaluation form and send it back. Do not schedule a second meeting to review it.

NOTE 2

Occasionally the cause for a compulsory termination interview may be conflict between two individuals. The pastor should carefully consider the basic well-being of both individuals involved. In the event that reconciliation is possible, a process to achieve that goal should have been implemented prior to the compulsory termination interview. If that attempt was unsuccessful, further attempts may be as well. However, it should be kept in mind that there is an obligation to make certain that the individual being terminated understands that he or she is still part of the parish community, and that if he or she does not, appropriate steps should be taken quickly to rectify that situation.

Record Keeping

Throughout the process we have stressed record keeping. The last thing needed by most pastors is more time devoted to maintenance of records. However, if the forms provided in this manual are duplicated, or adopted, and are completed immediately after each interview, very little time is required.

Good records are important from a number of perspectives.

1. Pastors have many meetings, and it is not easy to reconstruct the content of a meeting that may have happened six months ago.

2. A pastor may be transferred and adequate records will insure that the new pastor and staff will have an easier transition.

3. Only so much data can be covered in a given meeting. Careful records will allow the pastor to retain topics for future meetings.

Care should be taken to keep all personnel records in a secure place. Records of volunteers should be maintained with the same integrity as those of paid staff.

Volunteer Application Form

Mr.
Mrs.
Miss_____

First   Initial   Last   Spouse's Name

Address _____

Street or RFD   City   State   Zip

Employed at_____Department _____

Telephones _____ _____ _____

Home   Business   Extension

Education: High School ( ); College ( ); Major_____ Degree_____

Other Schooling or Special Training _____

Interests or Hobbies _____

Skills (be specific) _____

_____

Have you done volunteer work before? _____ What?_____

_____ Where? _____

Availability: Sun.   Mon.   Tues.   Wed.   Thurs.   Fri.   Sat.

Morning: _____

Afternoon:_____

Evening: _____

Weekly ( ); Twice Monthly ( ); Other _____

Volunteering through what organization? _____

_____

Who or what prompted you to volunteer? _____

_____

References: (Give full names and addresses)

1. _____

2. _____

3. _____

VI. Forming Volunteer Agreements

Agreement

It is often difficult to maintain a spirit of professionalism and goal orientation among volunteer staff. It is helpful at the outset to set a tone for the fact that certain standards of performance are expected and that certain levels of training should be sought within a reasonable time frame. The Agreement Form, which follows, should be completed for each ministry and signed by the volunteer and the pastor at the entry interview. It should be completed in duplicate: one copy is for the pastor and one should be given to the volunteer.

Feel free to adapt this form to the needs of your parish. It is recommended that the spirit of the statements at the end of the form be maintained. Each parish should review these with an attorney to be sure that they *do* limit liability and provide sufficient information to the volunteer.

Agreement Form

Position _____

Volunteer's Name _____

Address _____

City/Zip _____

Home Phone _____

Work Phone _____

Length of Term _____

Objectives and Estimated Completion Dates _____

_____

_____

_____

_____

_____

Training Required and Completion Date _____

_____

_____

_____

_____

SPENDING AUTHORIZATION
    1. Total budget for period_____ to_____
is $_____.

    2. Expenditures over $_____ must be approved by the pastor or _____

    3. Budget increases must be approved by _____

and the procedure for approval is _____

_____

_____

_____

EVALUATIONS
    An evaluation of the progress of your objectives will take place regularly. During your term, evaluations by the pastor will occur in the following months:

_____, 198_____   _____, 198_____
_____, 198_____   _____, 198_____
_____, 198_____   _____, 198_____

NOTIFICATION REQUESTED
    Please attempt to follow these guidelines:
    1. Notify rectory at least 48 hours ahead of time if you can't attend a meeting.

    2. Give *your immediate* supervisor at least three weeks' notice of a need for extended time off.

    3. Provide *your immediate* supervisor with a minimum of six weeks' notice if you wish to vacate your position.

PLEASE NOTE: I understand that the position I am accepting is strictly a volunteer position. I am not an employee of _____ Church and therefore I will not hold the church responsible for wages, workmen's compensation or expense reimbursement, except as covered in the budget projected above. I have no authority to spend money or authorize expenditures by anyone else on behalf of the church except as authorized explicitly by the pastor.

    I understand that the pastor may for cause replace me without notice prior to the expiration of my term.

Signature of Volunteer _____
Date _____
Signature of Pastor _____
Date _____

VII. First Steps

The Value of Paperwork

Coming Aboard

Rationale

Every pastor faces the inevitable responsibility of completing paperwork because he is a manager. The rationale for paperwork ordinarily falls into two categories.

a. Practical matters (business): these forms, memos, written duties are based on "need" and allow credibility and long-term accountability. Diocesan reports may not seem of imminent value on a local level to a pastor when he is facing deadlines and the responsibility of compiling the data and/or information. It is important that the long-term effects of this responsibility be remembered in that in time to come the data and records compiled now will, in fact, ease the burden and/or simplify the process for others.

b. Theological responsibility to provide honest records and in justice report and record specific occurrences for and about individuals of a sacramental and personal nature.

Kinds of Paperwork

The first type of paperwork usually is that which is forwarded from a higher level—diocesan, ordinarily. The immediate implications of this are not always clear at any given moment but the far-reaching effects are, in fact, quite clear.

The second segment is official documentation materials dealing with sacramental records, etc.

Finally, there are volunteers' records called for in their manual. This type of data ordinarily will provide a pastor with general background data, continuity and a basis for reflective judgment in fact rather than in memory. Pastors owe themselves and their parish staff and membership the best data retention possible on a continuing basis in order that, whatever final decisions are necessary, a documented record is on hand. It is ordinarily impossible to reconstruct accurately the interrelationships and dynamics of the staff when there is a transition to a new pastor. These general indicators would be very useful in continued staff and parish development.

Once a person has agreed to serve, care must be taken to bring him or her on board smoothly. In a later chapter we discuss training, support mechanisms and so on. Here, however, we recommend a series of steps intended to move the volunteer minister quickly into position to manage his or her area of responsibility.

Paperwork

In the review of interviewing procedures we made mention of the value of paperwork. Although it is difficult to sell this concept to a busy pastor, its importance can't be overstated. This section will again deal with forms, i.e., calendar and budget, that must be reviewed by the pastor. Some thoughts about the processing of paperwork are in order.

1. Prioritize the paperwork to be completed or reviewed. Develop a monthly file for forms to be completed and file them as much as two weeks before they're due. You can then work on them as time permits and still have enough flexibility to gather needed information on a timely basis.

2. Establish uniform procedures for the completion of forms that must be done regularly. Delegate the completion of such forms whenever possible so that you are taking full advantage of the expertise of your volunteer ministers.

3. Handle paper only once. Decide the who, how, when and where of its completion and move it off your desk.

4. Date each piece of material that requires a response from you as it comes into your office. Note a response date on the item and then meet it. Uncomplicated items should be answered immediately to avoid congestion.

5. Organize your desk, files and materials to allow for efficient and effective processing of paper.

6. Develop personnel and position files on all key staff—paid and volunteer. Use the personnel file for the application, performance appraisal forms and notes relating to performance. Use the position file for task related items such as goals, objectives, budgets, calendars, etc.

7. Insist that paid, or volunteer staff treat their paperwork with the same standards that you will be applying to yours.

Goals and Objectives

Parish leadership (staff and council) should develop goals on an annual basis. Each ministry area should have a goal for the coming year. This group (staff and council) may then state some specific objectives to be met on the way to attaining the goal. Alternatively they may leave the setting of objectives to the volunteer minister.

Once leadership has suggested goals and objectives, each minister should flesh out the objectives and review them with his or her peers and the pastor. These objectives then become crucial to the development of a work plan, calendar and budget.

If the minister in charge of a specific area is new to the job, then one of the following steps should be used.

1. If goals and objectives for this area exist, ask the minister to work with them for sixty days and then meet with the pastor to review changes which the minister may suggest. All changes should then be reviewed by the council.

2. If goals and objectives do not exist, council and staff (including the new minister) should work to immediately identify them. In no case should the minister begin to develop his or her own goals or objectives without the specific direction of the pastor/council process.

The development of goals and objectives should proceed as outlined in the following pages.

Setting Goals and Objectives for the Parish

Following is the outline of a process which has been used in many parishes and found to be most beneficial. Not only does the parish leadership develop goals and objectives, but it also develops a sense of unity, pride and ownership in the future of the parish.[9]

The PURPOSE of a planning session is twofold:

1. to establish a common sense of direction;

2. to define the specific steps to be taken in moving in such a direction.

A plan for any parish would set directions for logical and systematic development of the parish community in response to community needs.

PARTICIPANTS in the process should include parish council, committee chairpersons, staff (paid and volunteer), pastor and lay leadership as determined by council. The determination of additional lay leadership should be based on the ability of these people to bring to the session specific experience and insights regarding the parish.

TIME COMMITMENT is critical to the success of such a process. The time-frame for sessions is usually 7:30 to 10:00 on a Friday evening and from 9 A.M. until about 3 P.M. on a Saturday. Participants are asked to only agree to attend if they are able to participate in both sections of the process.

RESULTS from such a process include the following:

1. A parish mission statement

2. Goals for a specific period of time

3. Objectives for each goal

4. Person or committee responsible for implementation

5. Time-frame for completion

6. A monitoring and evaluation process

FOLLOW-UP to the plan is based on the ability of the parish council or staff to direct the development of the implementation process and require its review by council.

The agenda for such a session might be as follows:

FRIDAY
7:30 Opening prayer
7:45 Introductions and review of the Parish Mission Statement/Vision
8:15 Develop a purpose statement for planning session
9:00 Reflections on the parish as minister
9:45 Night prayer
10:00 Social

SATURDAY
9:00 Morning prayer
9:15 Leadership and parish life
(An opportunity to review the roles and responsibilities of council, committees and all staff positions)
10:00 Needs assessment
10:30 Priority list developed
11:00 Goal development
11:45 Break for lunch
12:45 Present goals
1:15 Develop objectives
2:30 Presentation of objectives
3:00 Following up on the process
3:15 How to publish the plan to the parish

Goals

A Goal is a clear statement of desired direction of activity in broad, general terms. It is the desired end result which is to be obtained when planning is complete. It can be a desired end state, a desired future condition of a desired norm. A goal can be defined as long term (5 years) or short term (1-2 years).

A GOAL statement has seven main characteristics:

1. It is a guide to action stated as a desired outcome, a result, a desired condition of state of affairs.

2. It is general in its direction.

3. It is challenging, exciting and inspiring to participant(s).

4. It calls for investment and involvement.

5. It may provide a time target.

6. It is directly tied to the purposes and goals of higher units in the organization.

7. It can be attained through a series of objectives and their strategies.

LEAD WORDS
The discussion, appreciation, assurance, belief, coordination, knowledge or improvement.

FORM FOR WRITING GOALS
The _____ + "what will you do" + for whom you will do it + when.
Example: The coordination of parish liturgical events for the advent season. This will be developed during September and October with implementation during the season.

Objectives

An Objective is a specific, time-oriented, and realistic statement of what the group or individual is going to do, who is going to do it, for whom, when, and how much is to be done. Objectives are the main intermediate results needed to obtain a goal. A good objective has eight main characteristics:

1. It begins with the word "to" and is followed by an action verb.

2. It produces a single key result when accomplished.

3. It specifies for or with whom an action is done.

4. It has a specific target date for accomplishment.

5. It is quantifiable and measurable—how much is to be done. It can be evaluated.

6. It is clear and understandable for all those involved.

7. It is realistic and attainable—considers present and anticipated resources.

8. It helps the group or individual achieve one or more of its stated goals.

LEAD WORDS
To write, compare, eliminate, establish, approve, identify, design.

OBJECTIVES FORM
To + action verb + specific task + from whom + when + who will do it.[10]

Work Plan

Once goals and objectives for an area have been developed, time should then be taken by each minister to develop a work plan.

1. List all objectives in order of starting date.

2. Develop strategies (steps to be taken) for each objective and place them under the objective in order of starting date. Note the completion date for each strategy as well.

3. Note dates under each strategy when components should be starting and ending.

4. Review the above with the pastor.

5. Once all objective and strategy schedules are approved, use a blank calendar, or a sheet of paper for each month of the year, to list strategy starting and ending dates.

6. Insert other dates on the calendar for specific events, meetings, etc., which will occur in your ministry area.

7. Present the calendar at the next council meeting for their input.

Budgets

In this age of accountability, every parish should have a budget development process. The process should be agreed upon by the council and should apply to all activities of the parish from full-time ministries to events that only occur once a year.

During the process of developing a ministry, the pastor should place substantial controls on spending. All requests for materials, supplies, etc. should be approved by the pastor.

Once staff and council have provided the minister with a goal and objectives, the minister will begin to develop strategies. Each one should be budgeted completely. The pastor should review these budgets as he reviews the calendar. The council should do the same. Once both have agreed, the budgets should be given to the parish finance committee for inclusion in an overall parish budget.

A process for monitoring these budgets should be put into place. As the number of volunteer ministries increases, the pastor will be hard put to monitor every expenditure against the amount approved.

It is also wise to set a maximum amount that can be spent by a minister at any one time. Any expenditure over that amount should be approved by the pastor.

Distinction Between Policy and Administration

As parish staffing expands there can be tension between those who develop policy and those who implement it. This situation can result in negatives ranging from a misunderstanding as to who is responsible for what to assumption of power by an individual who shouldn't have it. The information that follows is intended to assist the parish in determining the difference between items that are policy and those that are administration.

A *policy* is a guideline for action. It answers the question, "In what direction do we want to go?" A policy indicates the intent of the policy-making person or group.

Administration is the process of implementing policy. Administration works at answering the question, "How can we best implement this policy?" The administration attempts to implement the intent of the policy formulator.

In principle, the distinction between policy and administration is necessary for the implementation of shared responsibility. The application of this distinction to the church is new and in practice the distinction between what is policy and what is administration in the church is often fuzzy. One of the ongoing tasks of parish councils is to clarify the point where policy ends and administration begins.

The following is a list of types of policy statements, some sample policy statements and administrative steps. This list is not intended to be definitive or exhaustive.

1. **Law or Mandate of Directive**
Policy: The parish will require three two-hour sessions for baptismal preparation of parents requesting baptism for their children. Series will be offered four times yearly.
Administration/Implementation:
Recruiting and training of team members
Selecting background texts and materials
Scheduling time and place of sessions, etc.

2. **Recommendations or Encouragement**
Policy: Every woman parishioner is encouraged to be a member of the Catholic Woman's Club.

Administration/Implementation:
Membership drive
Publicizing drive and purpose of club
Welcoming prospective and new members

3. Public Statements of Position

Policy: Parish endorses the Campaign for Human Development

Administration/Implementation:
Recruiting donors
Publicizing activities
Distributing information

4. Setting Goals and Priorities

Policy: By December, 19_____ _____
Parish will have completed a self-study to determine a Vision and Mission Statement to give direction to the parish.

Administration/Implementation:
Determining method of self-study
Contacting outside resources
Overseeing the process

5. Establishing New Offices or Boards

Policy: A subcommittee of the liturgy committee is established with the goal of fostering vocations to the priestly and religious life.

Administration/Implementation:
Recruiting membership

Developing programs
Setting time lines

6. Establishing Requirements and Competency Criteria for Top-Level Personnel

Policy: The requirements for the position of associate pastoral minister:

- Must have degree in theology or equivalent
- Must be willing to work with all ages and a variety of aspects of parish life
- Must relate well to people and demonstrate willingness to cooperate with others in ministry

Administrative/Implementation:
Recruiting
Interviewing
Hiring
Training/Orientation
Termination

7. Approving Parish Budget

Policy: The parish council approves the annual budget for _____ Parish.

Administration/Implementation:
Writing checks
Banking funds
Providing for unplanned emergency expenses
Maintaining accounts

VIII. Training Volunteers

Principles

Often a parish community makes assumptions about either the preparation a person has for a ministry or the level of need for continued training once he or she has begun the ministry. These assumptions usually are the result of a lack of understanding of the types of training that parishes need to provide for all who serve in ministry in the parish. For this reason, we specify the types of training that are most helpful in parish communities not only to assist new volunteer ministers but also to support and further develop those whose involvement is over a longer period of time.

1. *Pastor's first responsibility* is to the spiritual development of volunteers, and to that end he needs to provide opportunities for spiritual development.

2. *Orientation* is helping persons prepare to do a ministry before they actually begin. For a committee, staff or council member, it may mean becoming familiar with recent records, minutes or activities. It is important that new members understand the operating norms, procedures and roles before they become involved. It may be a time for retreat with all members of the group focusing on roles, functions, relationships to Vision and the value of each individual.

3. *On the job ministry training* occurs while the person is engaged in the task. This should be intentional training with specific, established learning goals. It is never enough to team a new and old member of any group and assume that knowledge and experiences will be transmitted. Both need to know what the new member must learn and how a partner is able to assist.

4. *Continuing education* is growth and development that happens outside the regular duties of the ministry. It may be ongoing or concentrated in any given area of content or skill development (Scrip-ture, leadership, communication, decision making or human relations). It may be very specific training for a very specific aspect of the ministry.

5. *Training may occur on an individual or group basis* depending on the needs of both the individual and the group.[11]

How to Train the Volunteer

The first step in training volunteers is to determine what kinds of training are needed for each volunteer ministry. Ask persons who have formerly been involved in the volunteer ministry the following questions:

1. What would someone beginning this ministry need to know to do it well?

2. What kinds of skills would be useful in this ministry that persons aren't likely to have before they are recruited?

3. What experiences, training or resources have been helpful to you in this ministry?

4. What would you want to say to the person who follows you in this ministry?

5. What prayers/spiritual opportunities were most helpful?

Discover what training is being provided currently and see how well this covers the identified needs.

Determine what training is most needed and whether it must be done on an individual basis or whether a group of volunteers could participate.

Identify training resources in the community and in other churches in the diocese.

Don't overlook the possibility of providing training for persons whose ministry is beyond the local church if other training opportunities are not available to them.[12]

Information Form: Training
(This tool is used by the staff/pastor in training volunteers. It is useful in interviewing to secure information which will assist the staff/pastor in planning a good training program for the parishioners.[13])

    1. MINISTRY POSITION _____

    2. What would someone beginning this ministry position for the first time need to know, or need help with, in order to do the ministry well?

    3. What experiences, training or resources have been helpful to you as you have done this ministry?

    4. What would you want to say to the person who follows you in doing this ministry?

    5. What suggestions would you like to make on training volunteers?

    6. Other comments:

Interviewer _____ Date_____

IX. Supporting Volunteers

Guidelines for Supporting Volunteers

As the number and responsibilities of volunteers in ministry develop it is essential that these volunteers have the support of the pastor and other parish leadership. We have adopted some helpful suggestions that are presented in "The Church and Its Volunteers."[13] The suggestions place this responsibility on all who share leadership for the parish, not solely on the pastor.

The volunteers must be aware of the relationship between faith commitment, church membership and their ministry in the parish. The job description for each volunteer ministry must be clearly understood in light of the Vision of the parish. It is most beneficial to spend extra time in assuring full understanding of the two aspects and their interdependence. This allows the volunteers the opportunity to clarify any confusions that may exist.

Orientation sessions provide the forum for the obvious questions and concerns of practical nature to be asked. Training in specific skills or to broaden the base of knowledge should be provided under the direction of the pastor.

Private and public recognition for the volunteers acknowledges their contribution and reinforces the gratitude of the pastor and people.

Materials are essential to the work of any volunteer, and it is the responsibility of the pastor to assure that adequate supplies are available. The responsibility of the volunteer is to use materials carefully and study them thoroughly.

Volunteers in ministry should be clearly advised of the nature and amount of reimbursement that will be provided by the parish. The willingness of the parish to pay for a seminar or the mileage to a meeting is a real plus. So, too, the parish should offer help with day-to-day expenses incurred.

Volunteer ministers need to attend "update" sessions on a regular basis. During these a basic review of developments in each area of parish life is discussed.

The pastor should keep records of the accomplishments of each volunteer. These will assist him in providing recommendations should the volunteer wish to use them in seeking a paid position elsewhere.

Suggestions for Volunteer Recognition

Parish volunteers often are taken for granted. They, and the services they provide, often are unrecognized, unthanked and unsupported. They deserve our recognition and gratitude. The role of the volunteer in the life and ministry of the parish is an important one. Without such volunteers there probably would be no extensive ministry in our parishes.

Following is a list of ways to support and recognize volunteers and the work they do within the local parish, in the diocese and in the life of the community.

- Publish a list of persons who volunteer within the parish, diocese and/or deanery and distribute it to the parishioners, post it on the bulletin board and print it in the parish newsletter.
- Plan a liturgy around the theme of volunteer ministry.
- Plan a volunteer recognition dinner, invite all volunteers and honor them with certificates, awards and honors.
- Reimburse the out-of-pocket costs that volunteers incur as part of their volunteer ministries.
- Ask for a report.
- Send a birthday, anniversary, special occasion card.
- Provide a child care service to enable mothers and fathers of young children to volunteer.
- Keep challenging volunteers.
- Provide good orientation on the ministry training and continuing education opportunities.
- Give additional responsibility.
- Send newsworthy information about the volunteers to the local newspapers.

- Have a volunteer party.
- Create pleasant surroundings for the work and meetings.
- Take time to talk with volunteers and express appreciation for their efforts.
- Form volunteer support groups for sharing in joy, growth and prayer.
- Share the positive comments you hear about volunteers and their work.
- Provide scholarships and expense money for volunteers to attend training and continuing education workshops.
- Write personal thank you notes.
- Celebrate outstanding projects.
- Provide good resources.
- Praise volunteers to their friends.
- Provide opportunities for individual conferences.
- Maintain an accurate record of their training and work and be prepared to provide a reference for the volunteers when they seek employment or other volunteer ministries.
- Plan a volunteer-of-the-month celebration.
- Have a volunteer and family picnic.[14]

X. Supervisory Skills

Leadership should not be confused with what we refer to as supervisory skills. We deal here with leadership as one function of a range of skills. The basic elements of good supervision:

1. **Understanding the Vision.** Clearly you cannot direct others' activities effectively without knowing:

A. Where is the parish today?
B. Where is it going? (or where should it be going?)
C. Who needs to do what to make all, or a piece of it, happen?
D. How am I or those working for me accountable for our activities? (By measuring the degree of progress toward or deviation from the Vision.)

2. **Understanding Human Behavior.** All supervisors, to be successful, must be able to predict within reasonable limits the expected behavior of subordinates. Then there must be a plan for dealing with both successful and unsuccessful outcomes. Much of this can be instructive with certain supervisors, but many will think they can do it and cannot. They will need help in developing these skills.

3. **Leadership.** This is a truly rare quality if existent in any quantity within a person. It involves many of the other items mentioned here but also that rather mystical ability to serve the mix of things and know how much to push or pull and when to do which. It is mentioned rather than the average supervisor's skill of just going through the mechanics. More than anything else, leadership in our context today involves a heavy dose of Christian concern for the welfare of those being led.

4. **Organizational Ability.** The supervisor must have enough skill in this area to at least be able to organize materials relevant to the area, keep the work going to and through subordinates in an orderly way and still have enough personal organizational ability to find time for growth behavior such as planning and learning, in addition to fulfilling all obligations at home and work.

5. **Delegation.** The supervisor is not delegating if responsibility and accountability are not placed squarely upon the person who is to do the job. Often we give the impression that people should do specific tasks, but they keep coming back for approval every step of the way. This is not delegation; in fact, many times it results in more work.

True delegation means that you have defined the task and estimated properly a person's ability to do it, provided proper training and definition, and then nudged him or her out of the nest, only to be seen again if he or she senses a problem or when regular reporting times occur. Top executives spend ninety percent of their time supervising and ten percent doing tasks, while the lowest level of management only spends thirty percent of their time supervising and seventy percent of the time in task implementation.

6. **Goal Setting.** Most supervisors (except the very top) are on a two-way street. They participate in goal setting and objective design at the higher level of management and then must work with their staff to translate those into goals and objectives for those below.

7. **Evaluation.** We say it as often as we speak on management. Once you have put a person in a position to do a job, paid or volunteer, you owe it to that person, to the parish and to yourself to make sure that regular scheduled evaluations are an expected part of the job. Follow-through is critical.

8. **Planning.** Planning is the development of long range goals and objectives rather than the short term implementation of agenda developed elsewhere. It is helpful and motivating for people to know where we all are attempting to move and what potential we have to accomplish this.

9. **Decision Making.** The supervisor cannot put off decisions except on the most grave sort of things. The pastor must work with supervisors to illustrate the areas in which they can and must make decisions and provide them with some ideas on gaining input, reaching consensus where appropriate and, finally, on announcing and implementing decisions.

10. **Motivation.** Keep up a head of steam. It is a big mistake to confuse good supervision with good coaching. Good coaching is predominantly visceral in its use of motivational techniques. The type of motivation this engenders lasts about sixty seconds.

In a volunteer environment constructed for the long term, motivation is intellectual and spiritual. Go for head and soul commitment, not for programmed responses. People must understand the why of things and planners must not try to build Rome in a day. If these criteria aren't met, burn-out will occur and you will be running an out-patient clinic. Take breaks every few months. Send notes of praise to entire families for sharing Mom or Dad. Have public recognition events, awards, etc.

11. **Communication.** Utilize skills to the limit with no assumptions about what others hear or know. Train those who supervise to strive for open and honest lines of communication. It is crucial to success.

12. **Conflict.** Plan for it and plan on it. It will happen in ongoing relationships. Provide some training for staff supervisors in identifying and resolving conflict. Make an intervention process available at each level (but not the pastor as intervener unless all else fails). Provide ample opportunites through which conflict can be dealt with early and openly.

XI. Evaluation Procedures

Report and Evaluation of a Volunteer Ministry

The following form[15] is valuable when a volunteer is terminating the ministry involvement for any reason.

Questions provide valuable information for recruiting new volunteers and improving the processes used in support and training of current volunteers.

Frequently, the pastor or supervisor is unaware of some of the internal difficulties, needs or successes even when regular evaluations are provided. This information is made available in a format such as provided.

Report and Evaluation of a Volunteer Ministry

Name _____ Date_____

Name of Ministry Position _____

Term of the Position: From_____To_____

1. This ministry position has been satisfying for me because . . .

2. The major frustrations in this ministry position have been . . .

3. I used the following skills in this ministry position . . .

4. The training I received for this position included . . .

---

5. I felt supported in this position in the following ways . . .

6. I received the following resources which assisted me in this position . . .

7. I would have been able to do this ministry better if . . .

8. The highlights of this ministry for me have been . . .

9. The major accomplishments which have been achieved through this ministry include . . .

10. A person following me in this ministry position needs to know . . .

Please rate each of the following as it enabled you to do this ministry effectively and faithfully by placing an "X" in the appropriate column.

	Outstanding	Average	Inadequate
11. The way in which the position was interpreted and explained to me before I began	_____	_____	_____
12. The training I received for doing the ministry	_____	_____	_____

13. The support I received from the church   _____   _____   _____

14. The challenge and responsibility I felt in
doing this ministry   _____   _____   _____

15. The sense of importance the church places
on this ministry   _____   _____   _____

The following are about your future volunteer ministries. Please indicate your interests by placing an "X" in the appropriate column.

	Very Interested	Somewhat Interested	Would Like to Know More	No Interest
16. A new volunteer ministry position:				
a. In my church	_____	_____	_____	_____
b. In my community	_____	_____	_____	_____
c. In my deanery/diocese	_____	_____	_____	_____
d. In an ecumenical setting	_____	_____	_____	_____

17. Specific volunteer ministry opportunities I would like to explore:

18. Factors in my situation that would influence my next volunteer ministry position:
Schedule:

Transportation:

Other:

19. Additional Comments:

Annual Evaluation for Staff

An instrument or process similar to the one which follows is appropriate for use by the staff, council or a combination of the two in determining where the development of volunteer ministry currently has evolved with the Vision statement clearly in mind.

The subgroupings may need to be revised or the process used selectively by smaller parishes, but all of the key elements in the development of volunteer ministries have been included.[16]

Checklist for Evaluating the Volunteer Ministry Program

	Satisfactory	Needs Work

CHURCH'S MISSION STATEMENT
The church's mission statement is current and is providing guidance for the volunteer ministry program   _____ _____

VOLUNTEER MINISTRY POSITION DESCRIPTIONS
All volunteer ministry positions in the church have been identified   _____ _____

Position descriptions have been written for all volunteer ministries in the church   _____ _____

Each ministry position description is on file in a central location   _____ _____

Each ministry position description has been evaluated for accuracy and clarity and the necessary changes made   _____ _____

VOLUNTEERING IDENTIFICATION, MATCHING AND RECRUITMENT
Volunteer ministry questionnaires were used and were an effective tool in the volunteer ministry program   _____ _____

The following changes need to be made in the questionnaire:

_____

_____

The steps of identifying, matching and recruiting are well organized and effective   _____ _____

The involvement and effectiveness of volunteers have increased because of careful matching   _____ _____

The volunteer ministry program has been strengthened because of new efforts in training   _____ _____

SUPPORTING VOLUNTEERS
The volunteer ministry program has been strengthened because of more adequate support being given volunteers   _____ _____

Resources and facilities have been adequate for effective volunteer ministry   _____ _____

Additional resources which are needed have been identified and plans made to secure them   _____ _____

RECOGNITION OF VOLUNTEERS

Volunteers have been adequately recognized by the church for their ministries in the:

Local church   _____   _____

Wider church   _____   _____

Community   _____   _____

The most effective types of recognition have been:

_____

_____

Recognition of volunteers needs improvement in the following ways:

_____

_____

PERSONAL INFORMATION CARDS

Personal information cards have been completed for each church member   _____   _____

Personal information cards have been updated to include the most recent volunteer ministry   _____   _____

MINISTRY POSITION CARDS

Personal information cards have been completed for each volunteer ministry in:

The local church   _____   _____

The deanery and diocese   _____   _____

Ecumenical agencies and groups   _____   _____

Community agencies and groups   _____   _____

New members of the church have been considered for volunteer ministry positions   _____   _____

TRAINING VOLUNTEERS

Training opportunities have been provided for:

Orientation to ministry positions   _____   _____

On-the-ministry training   _____   _____

Continuing education   _____   _____

Training opportunities are needed in the following areas:

_____

_____

The most effective training opportunities have been:

_____

_____

COMPLETING VOLUNTEER MINISTRIES

Each volunteer has filled out the report and evaluation form at the completion of service

_____ _____

The group working on closure activities has met and interviewed:

Committees and groups prior to their final meeting of the year

_____ _____

Volunteers within the church at completion of their ministries

_____ _____

Volunteers involved in wider church-community ministries at the completion of their ministries

_____ _____

GUIDING THE VOLUNTEER MINISTRY PROGRAM

Task forces working on different components of the volunteer ministry program have been an effective way to implement the church's volunteer ministry program

_____ _____

If appropriate:

The administrative system of the team and task forces has worked well

_____ _____

The team and task forces have felt supported by the congregation

_____ _____

Plans for integrating new persons into the team and task forces are being made

_____ _____

Overall, the following could be said in evaluation of the volunteer ministry program:

_____

_____

XII. Spirituality and the Volunteer Minister

"Without me you can do nothing" (Jn 15:5).

As parishioners with a special call to volunteer ministry, the first and basic need of each person is to pray, both individually and with the staff. Yet there is a malaise about the importance of prayer in busy modern life, prayer that is essential to the personal fulfillment of men and women of faith. To become stronger in their prayer life, Christians need to experience the value and joy of union with the Father and the self-integration that accompanies this.

All staff meetings should focus on prayer, and specific periods or days of reflection should be established so that not only personal growth but the sense of trust and sharing can be nurtured among the people forming the staff.

What is prayer? What does it mean to me today? How can we pray together? How can prayer make me a better minister? All such questions are appropriate and even essential to the life and growth of people working together for and in church.

Some suggestions on creating a favorable environment for prayer:

1. An atmosphere of relaxation, warmth, friendship and mutual trust is important. Before the prayer experience, have a time of quiet. If possible, have seating in a circle or around a table. Use a candle. Begin sometimes with sharing coffee, donuts, something appropriate to the session. Include moments of silence. Encourage spontaneous prayer but do not pressure or pry. Allow people to be unique.

Prayer should be varied and thoughtful, with opportunitites for reflection, dialogue and sharing. Creative use of structured prayer can lead people gently into more spontaneous sharing.

2. Ask volunteer ministers to lead prayer. Clergy can do much to encourage lay persons to assume this responsibility by their own enthusiasm and prayerful presence.

3. Prayer with the Scriptures adds the dimension of "the mind of Christ." Encourage reflections on the Scripture passage chosen. One way to do this is to read the Scripture passage aloud, and then break into groups of two or three for discussion on what the Scripture passage meant to each person.

4. Integrate prayer with the liturgical cycle of the Church year. Use the "Liturgy of the Hours."

5. The celebration and sharing of the Eucharist binds in the unity of "the one bread," a visible sign of the community of faith they symbolize.

6. At least once a year, a day or weekend of renewal that is solely centered on spirituality should be a must for the entire staff.

Life in God's Service

Introduction

The following is adopted from the *Encyclopedia of Serendipity* by Lyman Coleman.[17] The intent of this and similar activities is to allow members of a group the time and process to reflectively identify and attribute the creative and positive strengths of members of the groups. It basically affords a way to tell others in the group what about them you find of special value in this group.

Life in God's Service

"Do not think of yourselves more highly than you should. Instead, be modest in your thinking, and each one of you judge himself according to the amount of faith that God has given him. We have many parts in the one body, and all these parts have different functions. In the same way, though we are many, we are one body in union with Christ and we are all joined to each other as different parts of one body. So we are to use our different gifts in accordance with the grace that God has given us. If our gift is to speak God's message, we must do it according to the faith that we have. If it is to serve, we must serve. If it is to

Group Structures for Team Building

Certain communication exercises work best in groups of two, others in groups of four, and others in groups of eight. This is the reason for the suggestions given for structuring of different types of groups for different purposes.

CONFIGURATION	BEST USE	RATIONALE
Twosome (face to face)	Beginnings. Introductions. Conversation starters. Interviews.	With one other person most people are fairly relaxed and self-confident. Listening is easy and feeling is close.
Foursome	Getting acquainted. Discussions. Affirming decisions.	Everybody has a chance to talk. No moderator is necessary.
Wagonwheel (four back to back in center. Four on the outside rotating every two minutes).	Quick, multiple introductions. Initiating discussions and getting everyone's opinions.	An already formed group of 8 or 10 can keep together, yet be on a one-to-one while getting acquainted.
Eightsome (circle of eight)	Non-verbals are clear. Closing discussions. Leader required. Projects. Problem solving.	People work together in a support work over a long period of time. Will feel safe, protected and go into real depth.

teach, we must teach. If it is to encourage others, we must do so. Whoever shares what he has with others, must do it generously; whoever has authority, must work hard; whoever shows kindness to others, must do it cheerfully'' (Rom 12:3–8).

WARM-UP

To what degree do you feel strong or weak in the various spiritual gifts? (Read over the Scripture passage; then rank yourself from 1 to 10 on each of the spiritual gifts—1 being very weak and 10 being very strong. For instance, on the gift of "speech" you might circle number 3 because you feel that you are rather weak in communicating the Gospel verbally.)

Speak God's Message (speech)
God has given me a gift for communicating the Gospel. When I explain the good news, God seems to use my words to bring insight and understanding about his grace.

1 2 3 4 5 6 7 8 9 10

Serve (service)
God has given me a special knack for helping out when a need arises. I am sensitive to other people and find it easy to respond to their needs.

1 2 3 4 5 6 7 8 9 10

Teach (teaching)
God has given me a skill for helping others to learn. I am good at getting other people motivated.

1 2 3 4 5 6 7 8 9 10

Encourage Others
God has given me the disposition to see the best in others. I find it easy to compliment people—to point out their strengths, to "call forth" their best.

1 2 3 4 5 6 7 8 9 10

Generosity
God has given me a freedom to share myself with others. I find it easy to give, to reach out, to touch and care whenever there is a need.

1 2 3 4 5 6 7 8 9 10

Authority (leadership)
God has given me a gift for organization. I can get things done. I find it easy to take responsibility and direct others.

1 2 3 4 5 6 7 8 9 10

Kindness
God has given me the ability to be compassionate, warm and tender whenever someone is in trouble or needs help. I can enter into people's pain—feel with them—and minister.

1 2 3 4 5 6 7 8 9 10

GOING DEEPER

1. What gifts have the members of __(name of group)__ shown during the __(period of time)__ ? (On the left write the names of the people in your group. Then think over the list of "gifts" and jot a gift beside each name. For instance, for Tom you might put down "speech" because with his explanation you really understand the Gospel. For Bea you might put down "encouragement" because she has been the one to call forth the best in you.)

Name   Gift

_____   _____

_____   _____

_____   _____

_____   _____

How To Enable the Best in Each Other

The purpose of teams, staff or small groups is to help each other reach his or her full potential.

The way this is done is called ENABLING. The word ENABLE means to pull forth from, to call forth, to allow to emerge, to realize the potential of. This is what team is all about.

Most people realize about ten percent of their potential. The other ninety percent lies beneath a pile of fears, failures, broken dreams, painful childhood memories and guilt feelings that add up to make us feel we are not going to make it in anything we do. With that kind of outlook, we definitely will not.

This is where team, staff and small groups come in. In the company of loving people, we are able to grow in harmony with and complement the gifts of our companions.

Three Levels of Sharing

All of us yearn for fellowship where we can feel a oneness and call forth the best in each other—in other words, to minister to one another as the body of Christ. Before this can happen we must run the risk of sharing a little of ourselves.

One of the best ways to build a team is to ask the group to evaluate their experiences according to the three levels of sharing: (1) mouth to mouth, (2) head to head, (3) heart to heart.

The mouth-to-mouth sharing employs conversational doodling—the weather, the function of the job. The head-to-head sharing is more serious in that it is exchanging ideas and concepts—but the exchange is strictly of ideas detached from the persons. The heart-to-heart sharing lets the other person know where you stand in relation to the ideas and how you feel about him or her on the inside.

Some Tips on Team Building

1. When a person is willing to share how he or she feels about what is said or decided, don't interrupt.

2. Don't probe. There is a thin line between listening and probing. To listen is to enable a person to say all that he or she wishes to say. A probing question takes the initiative away from the person.

3. Don't give advice.

4. Don't judge. At times, the group will disagree on sensitive areas of life-style, theology and outlook.

Remember, to enable is to call forth the best in another person, to see the best in that person and to affirm the best in the person.

A SELECTED BIBLIOGRAPHY ON "SPIRITUALITY"

Documents of Vatican II, ed. by Walter Abbott, S.J., America Press, 1966.

Meeting God in Man, Ladislas Boros, S.J., Image Books, 1971.

Courage To Pray, Anthony Bloom, Paulist Press, N.Y., 1973.

The Father Is Very Fond of Me, Ed Farrell, S.J., Dimension Books, 1975.

Prayer Is Hunger, Ed Farrell, Dimension Books, 1974.

Face to Face With God, Jacques Loew, Paulist Press, 1977.

Reaching Out, Henri Nouwen, Doubleday, 1975.

Maintaining Relationships Within a Team

Development of a Faith Community

1. Pray together regularly.

● Not just a quick rote prayer or a routine sharing that is the same pattern each time.

● Vary prayer experiences.

● Allow time for sharing that will gradually deepen.

● Slowly deepen the prayer experiences so that you have the opportunity to grow together.

2. Regularly share your experience of ministry—NOT a reporting session!

● Share both successes and failures.

● Talk about where the Lord is in that experience.

● Look at the experiences and discover what you can learn from them to make your ministry richer.

3. Evaluate your team meetings. Regularly provide an opportunity for team members to share how they are feeling about the way the team meeting is going.

4. Take seriously any concern (no matter how trivial it may seem to you) a team member brings to you. Don't brush off someone's fears, etc., with comments like "Give it time!" or "That always happens to me, too."

5. At regular intervals assess the learning needs of the team.

6. Be sensitive to AND attend to things that need healing and reconciliation as the team works together. Don't avoid conflict. It doesn't go away.

7. Be open as a leader to allow the team to influence what you are doing as a team.

● Share expectations.

● Know the non-negotiables, make them clear, and remain firm.

● Allow the group as much as possible to plan the direction the team will move in.

8. Be prepared for meetings.

● Prepare agenda and give to people ahead of time.

● Start on time.

● End on time unless *everyone* agrees to go longer.

9. Keep a file.

● Record decisions.

● Always name who is accountable for carrying out decisions and keep a record.

● Follow through with promises.

● At beginning of each meeting QUICKLY review previous decisions and how things are moving with them.

10. Celebrate together.

● Be sensitive to little things like birthdays, etc.

● Allow some time for socializing.

● Celebrate successes, and failures, too.

Communication and the Development of Teams

We are looking for a place where we can
exercise trust in depth;
where listening, receiving, and giving
take place in a communion.
We are looking for a place of genuine
significance and identity,
where life and people and vocation
can be seen and experienced in
proper perspective.
We are looking for a place where acceptance
isn't earned by donning masks,
where relationships are genuine,

where struggle and faith are valid . . .
We are looking for a place where silly,
stupid, subtle religious images are
challenged, surrendered, changed . . .
Where is that place?
We are looking for a place like that . . .

1. Read the above poem.

2. Imagine "that place" in part is your ministry team.

3. What are the implications for your team if that is true?

4. Share (a) the thoughts, and then (b) the feelings you experienced, remembering you are the person in charge of that team.[18]

XIII. Time Management and Delegation

Time Management

One of the most critical areas of volunteer service is time management. Since all volunteers will have other areas of their life that are primary, the volunteer ministry is, by definition, secondary. The time spent on it must be used extremely well.

The pastor should control the biggest time wasters—meetings. From initial interviews to team meetings, all agendas should be pre-arranged and timed out. If an agenda item runs over, take steps to table it until it can be addressed with more chance of conclusion.

At the first team meeting, the pastor should ask the group to agree on some ground rules.

1. All meetings will start precisely on time.

2. All agendas, with times for each item indicated, will be sent to the team one week ahead of time.

3. Each team member should give a brief written report on his or her area to the pastor on time for inclusion with the agenda distributed (one week before the meeting).

4. Areas of ministry where projects or programs are operating successfully, i.e., according to plan, should not be discussed in detail at staff meetings. Care should be taken, however, to acknowledge the fact that the programs are operating effectively and to recognize the people responsible. From time to time, it may be appropriate to include a briefing on a program that has not been discussed in a good while.

5. Questions and answers on ministry reports should be brief and to the point.

6. Individual comments, suggestions or questions can be asked outside of the meeting time.

7. End the meeting precisely on time.

The following materials should be reviewed by the pastor with individual ministers as part of the early stages of their training program. They should be reviewed by the team on a semi-annual basis at a meeting specifically intended to review use of time.

1. How To Use Time Effectively

2. Strategies in Dealing With the Management of Time

3. Delegation

There will be plenty of opportunity for staff members to put these principles into play as they begin to manage the activities of others. However, like speed reading, one must constantly strive for improvement or begin to lose the discipline.

It is the pastor's responsibility to constantly stay aware and keep others aware of the value of time.

Strategies for Effective Time Management

The following suggestions will provide basic guidelines for a more effective use of time.

Understand the parish Vision and the relationship of the special ministry to that Vision. Set goals and objectives in the specific ministry area to give orderly development to the work being done and to ensure that the individuals involved are able to observe accomplishments and become aware of areas where greater effort and direction is needed.

Know and be comfortable in the leadership style of the pastor as well as one's own leadership style. To be struggling against the leadership is counter-productive and exhausting.

Ministry by definition is that which is done in the Lord's name in response to the needs of his people. If we accept the definition we *accept importance of the work we are about* and that the amount we do may not be as significant as the quality of what is completed. It is sometimes assumed that one's effectiveness is equal to the volume of work one accomplishes when, in fact, the contrary may be true.

Organize each day's activities. Make a list of what is to be done in order of importance and then begin. Sometimes we waste a good deal of time doing little "busy work" jobs when some very essential (and time-consuming) task is deferred.

Few volunteer ministers will have the leisure of large blocks of uninterrupted time. For this reason it is not logical to defer projects until "there's time" or "the pressure is off." Once the volunteer has a clear understanding of a responsibility *the best approach is a direct one* even if that means breaking a project into smaller segments that can be reasonably accomplished in the time available.

Interruptions, phone calls, meetings, and many other day-to-day occurrences take time from busy schedules. Once the volunteer minister accepts these as part of and not intrusions on the ministry, the strain and drain are minimized and energy is substantially more.

The volunteer minister, by virtue of the responsibilities he or she has accepted, has a share in the development of the parish community. The volunteer needs to *actively involve as many people as possible* in the work of the ministry. Knowing how to delegate and what to delegate are topics covered later in the manual.

All too often poorly planned meetings become the beginning of a poorly implemented program. *A clear agenda, good leadership, and specific assignments,* as well as *beginning and ending on time,* create a positive and enthusiastic approach to a program. These steps save time that can be very valuable to the ministry. The pastor and all who work with the ministry should realize that the time is volunteered and must jealously guard any drain on the effective use of time or energies of the volunteer.

Managing Time

Someone once explained that there are three ways to focus time: (1) save time, (2) control time, and (3) make more time. Below are some examples in each of these categories that should help volunteer ministers to more productively manage time.

TIME SAVERS

- Plan meetings to begin and end on time, and stick to a pre-published agenda.
- Highlight materials as they are read so that later rereading focuses on needed or pertinent information.
- Develop a "to read" file and keep materials "for reading" on hand so that when the few moments present themselves the material is available.
- Prepare 31 file folders and number them 1 through 31. Reports, agendas, etc., for a specific date should be dropped in that file and thus be readily at hand as needed.

CONTROLLING TIME

- Be sensitive to deadlines on reports and agendas.
- Keep track of what volunteers working for and with you are doing.
- Avoid putting off until tomorrow what could be done today.
- Be able to say "No" to avoid over-commitment and the stress it creates.
- Set high standards but do not create the atmosphere that takes all the joy out of team work.

MAKING MORE TIME

- Plan ahead instead of being in the position of always catching up.
- Learn good communication skills.
- Share the implementation of programs or projects with other volunteers.
- Organize projects so that people do not duplicate tasks.
- Be grateful for the efforts of those who volunteer.
- Develop guidelines to support the programs and give clear direction.

Delegation

Delegation is the carrying out of a decision by a person other than the person who made it. It is also the assigning of responsibility and authority to others, making them accountable for the results.

Elements of delegation include the power to act (the authority), the placement of full responsibility for implementation and assignment of accountability in a way that is fully understood.

The method of delegation should be: defining what is to be done, the standard of performance, assigning the target dates, limits of authority of the recipient, all relevant information, follow-up process with intermediate reports required, and clear outcome expectation.

Essentials in Making the Delegation

Effective delegation requires a kind of communion between the pastor and the staff. It is one thing to delegate and simply expect the assignment to be carried out well. It is quite another thing to set the stage for it and to build in helps that will greatly enhance the likelihood of success. Among

How to Spring the Time Trap

Below are listed the time wasters most commonly encountered. To assist the reader in analyzing personal time wasters, possible causes and solutions are suggested for each. These are not intended to be exhaustive, but merely to serve as guidelines for further diagnosis. Causes and solutions tend to be personal, while the time wasters themselves are universal in nature.[19]

Time Waster	Possible Causes	Solutions
Lack of planning	Failure to see the benefit	Recognize that planning takes time, but saves time in the end
	Action orientation	Emphasize results, not activity
	Success without it	Recognize that success is often in spite of, not because of, methods
Lack of priorities	Lack of goals and objectives	Write out goals and objectives. Discuss priorities with subordinates
Over-commitment	Broad interests	Say "No"
	Confusion in priorities	Put first things first
	Failure to set priorities	Develop a personal philosophy of time. Relate priorities to a schedule of events
Management of crisis	Lack of planning	Apply the same solutions as for lack of planning
	Unrealistic time estimates	Allow more time. Allow for interruptions
	Problem orientation	Be opportunity oriented
	Reluctance of subordinates to break bad news	Encourage fast transmission of information as essential for timely corrective action
Haste	Impatience with detail	Take time to get it right. Save the time of doing it over
	Responding to the urgent	Distinguish between the urgent and the important
	Lack of planning ahead	Take time to plan—it repays itself many times over
	Attempting too much in too little time	Attempt less, delegate more
Paperwork and reading	Knowledge explosion	Read selectively. Learn speed reading
	Computeritis	Manage computer data by exception
	Failure to screen	Remember to filter. Delegate reading to subordinates
Routine and trivia	Lack of priorities	Set and concentrate on goals. Delegate non-essentials

	Over-surveillance of subordinates	Delegate, then give subordinates their head. Look to results, not details or methods
	Refusal to delegate; feeling of greater security dealing with operating detail	Recognize that without delegation it is impossible to get anything done through others.
Visitors	Enjoyment of socializing	Do it elsewhere. Meet visitors outside. Suggest lunch if necessary. Hold stand-up conferences
	Inability to say "No"	Screen. Say "no." Be unavailable. Modify the open-door policy
Telephone	Lack of self-discipline	Screen and group calls. Be brief
	Desire to be informed and involved	Stay uninvolved with all but the essentials. Manage exceptions
Meetings	Fear of responsibility	Make decisions without meetings
	Indecision	Make decision even when some facts are missing
	Over-communication	Discourage unnecessary meetings. Convene only those needed
	Poor leadership	Use agendas. Stick to the subject. Prepare concise minutes as soon as possible
Indecision	Lack of confidence in the facts	Improve fact-finding and validating procedures
	Insistence on all the facts—paralysis of analysis	Accept risks as inevitable. Decide without all the facts
	Fear of the consequences of a mistake	Delegate the right to be wrong. Use mistakes as a learning process
	Lack of rational decision-making process	Get facts, set goals, investigate alternatives and negative consequences, make decision and implement it
Lack of delegation	Fear of subordinates' inadequacy	Train. Allow mistakes. Replace if necessary
	Fear of subordinates' competence	Delegate fully. Give credit. Insure growth to maintain challenge.
	Work overload on subordinates	Balance the workload. Staff up. Reorder priorities.

the essentials that must be incorporated by the pastor as delegator are these:

- Explain the problem or project to the volunteer minister.
- Indicate to the specific volunteer minister what is to be done and what are the limitations.
- Establish the time-frame and what the best outcome would be.
- Make known your standards and expectations.
- Assure the volunteer minister of your availability for input or guidance.
- Build the necessary authority into the delegated task(s).
- Arrange informal interim meetings for periodic discussion and evaluation of the delegated project.
- Provide for the final report on the project or program.

Barriers to Delegation

The essential tool for the pastor to use in managing his time is delegation. Yet this tool is rarely used well. Its necessity is rarely understood. There are critical barriers to effective delegation in the delegator, the delegatee and the situation. The lists below itemize several problems already examined along with a number of others, some meriting special comment.[20]

BARRIERS IN THE DELEGATOR
Preference for operating
Demand that everyone know all the details
"I can do it better myself" fallacy
Lack of experience in the job or in delegating
Insecurity
Fear of being disliked
Refusal to allow mistakes
Lack of confidence in subordinates
Perfectionism leading to over-control
Lack of organizational skill in balancing workloads
Uncertainty over tasks and inability to explain
Disinclination to develop staff
Failure to establish effective controls and to follow up

BARRIERS IN THE DELEGATEE
Lack of experience
Lack of competence

Avoidance of responsibility
Over-dependence on the pastor
Disorganization
Overload of work
Immersion in trivia

BARRIERS IN THE SITUATION
One-man show policy
No toleration of mistakes
Critical nature of decisions
Urgency, leaving no time to explain
Confusion in responsibilities and authority
Understaffing

What Is Reverse Delegation?[21]

Reverse delegation occurs when the person to whom a responsibility has been given manipulates the delegator into reaccepting responsibility for the project or program. In this way the delegatee attempts to shirk responsibility.

Why Reverse Delegation Takes Place

At least six reasons that reverse delegation takes place are identified as:

1. The staff person wishes to avoid a task. It is easier to ask the pastor to decide for himself. Asking the pastor is a way of sharing if not shedding the responsibility and, over a long period of time, it becomes a habit of dependence. To break the habit, simply refuse to decide for the staff members. Ask simple questions such as, "What is your recommendation?"

2. The staff member is afraid of criticism, especially negative, unreasonable or public criticism. Constructive criticism should be offered in private.

3. The staff member lacks confidence which clearly comes from experience and knowledge. To develop it requires more than telling a staff member that he or she is good. He or she must be given experience with increasingly more difficult problems to help his or her sense of confidence grow.

4. The staff member lacks necessary information and resources to accomplish the task. No re-

sponsibility should be delegated without requisite tools and authority.

5. The pastor wants to be needed. This attitude is impossible to hide from the staff. The pastor may feel that making staff decisions himself demonstrates his indispensability.

6. The pastor is unable to say "No" to requests for help. The trend toward participative management has encouraged pastors to think in terms of support and assistance to their staff. The pastor who is unable to say "no" invites reverse delegation.

Appendix

This manual in its original form was developed for and with the Pastoral Alliance of Steubenville, Ohio as the working format for the development of the centrality model in the parish. The entire theory and implementation model for this is found in *The Ministering Parish* by Robert R. Newsome published by Paulist Press.

The materials which follow are letters and documents which were presented to the diocese and parishes as an introduction to and explanation of the Alliance.

They are incorporated here as samples of materials which serve as models for future reference.

To God's People in Southeastern Ohio:

I want to thank you for all that you have done in responding to the Church's call for renewal. I am especially proud that what you have accomplished has been rooted in Faith and prayer. Always we must remember that it is in the Spirit of Jesus that parishes are renewed.

Our world is so broken. Our brothers and sisters in the human family are so threatened, so alienated from one another. God is calling us as Church to build His Kingdom in this world to replace war with peace, hatred with love, injury with pardon, sin with justice.

To accomplish God's will we must be strong as Church. We must use the gifts and talents that are found not just in the priests and religious but in all God's People.

The parish is where Catholics experience Church. The way parish is presently shaped, however, is for a different age than ours. For the New Vision we need new structures to allow lay women and men to share with their priests decision-making and ministry.

Through RENEW and other programs of parish renewal we are growing in awareness of what Jesus means parish to be. It will be an ongoing struggle, however, to make that dream a reality. In our diocese some priests have bonded themselves together for prayer and study to search deeper into the ways of renewal. Together and with people in their parishes they have worked out a Faith Vision, they have undertaken programs for spiritual formation of parish leaders, they are developing ways to facilitate a more active participation of laity in the life and mission of the Church.

It is my fond hope that what has been experienced and learned by the Pastors of the Alliance may be shared by pastors and faithful in parishes throughout the Diocese.

This handbook is a move in that direction. It is the fruit of much research on the part of the Alliance of Pastors. Volunteers are crucial to the mission of our parishes. This manual is filled with wisdom and practical directions for finding and nurturing volunteers. I trust it finds wide readership.

Your brother in Christ,
Most Reverend Albert Ottenweller
Bishop of Steubenville

Dear Parishioners:

On a crisp Saturday filled with colored leaves and corncobs twelve Pastors were called together by the Bishop. We met, unclear as to our purpose but sure that the Bishop, in the spirit of Vatican Council II, called us together for the good of the parishes.

Heeding the call of the church to restructure, to rebuild, we twelve Pastors agreed to support and to challenge one another as we began to experience Christ more fully and so developed the Pastoral Alliance.

We reflected on the mission of the church to build up the body of Christ and realized we, as Pastors, are only individuals. We saw clearly that, through Baptism, our people are called in union with one another to build the Body of Christ.

Our common effort made us aware that our parishes could experience the same growth and awareness.

We now invite you to share as volunteer ministers, to gather people together, to nourish, to inspire, to reach out in ministry and mission, calling people to become fully human and alive in Christ.

This manual is set in faith with the sole purpose of bringing you, the parishioners, into the active life of the church.

Yours in Christ,

Historical Perspective

In response to Vatican II's concept of the church as "the people of God" in *Lumen Gentium,* new concepts, new terminology, new attitudes, and new practices must be incorporated into the life of the church. Since the needs and wants of people change, the church must be so structured to meet these needs in the most viable manner.

When Bishop A. Ottenweller came to the Diocese of Steubenville in 1977, he brought with him a Vatican II vision of what the church should be in modern times. His goal was to implement this vision in the parishes of our diocese. In June 1979, he called together 16 Pastors and challenged them to assist him exploring, devising and implementing new structures and processes geared to meet present and future needs in our parishes. Of this group, 12 men bonded themselves into an "Alliance of Pastors" dedicated to support, to prayerful study, and to be accountable to each other in striving to meet this challenge.

This Alliance came together for the first time in September 1979, with Fr. Peter Campbell as facilitator and Sr. Carol Gross as Executive Secretary. Meeting bi-monthly, this group began by sharing each member's own faith story and vision of the church. The result of this first phase was the writing of a "corporate" parish Vision statement.

The second phase was a determination of "corporate" challenge to the Pastors of the Alliance. As a result of our own corporate vision and challenge, Pastors began calling forth potential leaders in their parishes to develop a similar vision and challenge. As the Pastors learned the necessary skills for Pastoral leadership, Sister Carol developed and conducted lay leadership programs in the parishes of the Alliance. The result of phase two was a need to concern ourselves with staff development and restructuring.

Beginning in the fall of 1981, the energies of the Alliance were centered on Volunteer Ministry in every aspect. During this period the Volunteer Manual was developed under the guidance of William J. Bannon and Sr. Suzanne Donovan.

The final phase of the Alliance goals is that of Mission to the World, the elements and processes still to be clearly defined by the Pastors.

Diocese of Steubenville
Pastoral Renewal Alliance
Statement of Vision of the Church

The church is the New Covenant people of God, gathered in community under the leadership of the hierarchy, to worship the Lord and to celebrate His presence in the world. Its mandate is to keep alive and to faithfully proclaim the message of Jesus Christ.

The church, led by the Spirit, is a pilgrim people whose hope is in Christ and whose goal is the realization of the Kingdom. It receives its life from the sacraments. It is a Christ-centered community of faith, hope and love, committed to enabling all people to reach their God-given potential, always in process of becoming more fully human, more fully alive.

The basis of this community is faith in Jesus Christ as Son of God and Savior of mankind, anchored in hope and held together by love. It is called to teach, to minister, to console, to affirm, to reconcile, challenging people to respond to the Father's love in prayer, service, and Eucharistic worship. The church's ultimate goal is to bring about a kingdom of peace, justice and love.

Corporate Challenge

We are pastors, so we are challenged and commissioned

To gather people together, enabling them to become a faith community;

To listen to and to understand the needs of people (parish and area) by our individual and corporate presence, providing processes of dialogue and use of available resources;

To instill and foster in the people an awareness of being church;

114

To provide nourishment for the parish as a faith community. This is accomplished through liturgical worship and proclamation of the Word with the community, fortified by discerning prayer and study of Scripture;

To inspire and motivate the people to reach out in ministry and mission and to affirm them in their ministry;

To challenge the parish to minister to the needs of the community and to evangelize the marginal and alienated, calling all people to become more fully human, more fully alive;

To initiate processes of parish organization through involvement of Pastor and people in:

a. discernment of gifts
b. identification of leaders
c. formation of leaders
d. commission of leaders
e. involvement of total community

NOTES

1. *The Decree on the Apostolate of the Laity,* United States Catholic Conference, Washington, D.C., 1967.

2. *The American Catholic Laity,* United States Catholic Conference, Washington, D.C., 1980.

3. *The Ministry of Volunteers,* "The Church and Its Volunteers," Office of Church Life and Leadership, United Church of Christ, Winston-Salem, N.C., 1979.

4. *Whatsit,* Parish Evaluation Project, 1307 South Wabash, Chicago, Illinois 60605, 1980.

5. *Models of the Church,* Avery Dulles, Image Books, Garden City, N.Y., 1978.

6. *The Parish Development Process,* Marvin T. Judy, United States Catholic Conference, Washington, D.C., 1980.

7. *Hope Is an Open Door,* Mary Luke Tobin, Abingdon Press, Nashville, Tenn., 1981.

8. *Basic Tools for Recruitment of Volunteers,* Voluntary Action Centers, Chicago, Illinois 60603.

9. *The Practical Guide for Parish Councils,* William J. Rademacher, Twenty-Third Publications, 1979.

10. *The Ministry of Volunteers,* "Training Volunteers," Office for Church Life and Leadership, United Church of Christ, Winston-Salem, N.C., 1979.

11. *The Ministry of Volunteers,* "The Church and Its Volunteers," Office for Church Life and Leadership, United Church of Christ, Winston-Salem, N.C., 1979.

12. *The Ministry of Volunteers,* "Training Volunteers," Office for Church Life and Leadership, United Church of Christ, Winston-Salem, N.C., 1979.

13. *The Ministry of Volunteers,* "The Church and Its Volunteers," Office for Church Life and Leadership, United Church of Christ, Winston-Salem, N.C., 1979.

14. *The Ministry of Volunteers,* "Supporting Volunteers," Office for Church Life and Leadership, United Church of Christ, Winston-Salem, N.C., 1979.

15. *The Ministry of Volunteers,* "Completing Volunteer Ministries," Office for Church Life and Leadership, United Church of Christ, Winston-Salem, N.C., 1979.

16. *The Ministry of Volunteers,* "The Church and Its Volunteers," Office of Church Life and Leadership, United Church of Christ, Winston-Salem, N.C., 1979.

17. *Encyclopedia of Serendipity,* Lyman Coleman, Mennonite Publishing House, Scottdale, Pa., 1978.

18. *Communication Skills* by Robert Bolton, Ph.D., published by Ridge Consultants, 1980.

19. *The Time Trap,* R. Alec MacKenzie, McGraw-Hill Paperbacks, New York, 1972.

20. *Ibid.*